LIVING ON THE EDGE
FOXES

Acknowledgments

The quote in chapter one is taken from the book *The Little Prince* by A. de Saint Exupery, New York: Harcourt, Brace and World, Inc., 1943.

Parts of Chapter 2 first appeared in a different form in the book *Red Fox: The Catlike Canine,* by J. D. Henry, Smithsonian Institution Press, Washington, D.C. (1986).

Parts of Chapter 4 first appeared in a different form in the article "Home Again on the Range" by J. D. Henry, in *Equinox* 13 (1995): 46-53.

Suzanne Henry has provided helpful editing for my writing as long as I have been writing about foxes, and this book is certainly no exception. I thank her for her insights and steadfast support.

Thanks to Keith Jensen from the Nova Scotia Museum for his careful review of the text. It was done with the same thoroughness as is evident in his own red fox research.

Thanks to Barbara Harold at NorthWord Press for her support throughout the project.

Photography © 1996: Tom & Pat Leeson, Front Cover, 18, 22, 61; Richard Day/Daybreak Imagery, 1,38-39; Alan G. Nelson/Dembinsky Photo Associates, 4; Alan & Sandy Carey, Chapter openings head shot, 6, 34-35, 70; Joe McDonald/Tom Stack & Associates, 8-9; Dominique Braud/Dembinsky Photo Associates, 11; Art Wolfe, 12, 21, 28-29, 31, 36, 42, 84, 104, 117, 123, 130, 134, Back Cover; Joe McDonald/Bruce Coleman, Inc., 14; J. David Henry, 17; John Shaw, 24; Gary Schultz/The Wildlife Collection, 27, 107, 112-113, 127; D. Robert Franz/The Wildlife Collection, 32, 92; Jim Brandenburg/Minden Pictures, 40, 54, 58-59, 62-63, 68, 73, 82, 87, 120, 128; Wayne Lynch, 44-45, 65, 74-75, 106, 110-111; Mike Couffer/Bruce Coleman, Inc., 47, 48-49; Erwin & Peggy Bauer/Bruce Coleman, Inc., 50, 76, 78, 80-81, 133; Jeff Foott/Tom Stack & Associates, 52-53; Larry Brock/Tom Stack & Associates, 57; Laura Riley/Bruce Coleman, Inc., 90-91, 102; Bill Lea/Dembinsky Photo Associates, 94-95; Jen & Des Bartlett/Bruce Coleman, Inc., 97; Gary Meszaros/Dembinsky Photo Associates, 100-101; Tom Brakefield/Bruce Coleman, Inc., 109; Barbara Gerlach/Dembinsky Photo Associates, 115; Gary Meszaros/Bruce Coleman, Inc., 118; Michio Hoshino/Minden Pictures, 124-125, 126; Michael H. Francis, 136-137.

NorthWord Press, Inc.
P.O. Box 1360
Minocqua, WI 54548

Design by Kenneth Hey

For a free catalog describing our audio products, nature books and calendars, call **1-800-356-4465**, or write Consumer Inquiries, NorthWord Press, Inc., P.O. Box 1360, Minocqua, Wisconsin 54548.

Library of Congress Cataloging-in-Publication Data
Henry, J. David.
      Foxes : living on the edge / by J. David Henry.
          p.   cm.—(Wildlife series)
       ISBN 1-55971-568-5 (pbk.)
       1. Foxes—North America   I. Title   II. Series: Wildlife series
      QL737.C22H445 1996
      599.74'442—dc20   96-13250

Printed in Singapore

LIVING ON THE EDGE
FOXES

by J. David Henry

NorthWord
NORTHWORD PRESS, INC.
Minocqua, Wisconsin

To Suzanne

A life shared

from

Fontana Delle Tartarughe

to

Turtle Island

TABLE OF CONTENTS

EARLY MORNING FOX WATCHING

 Dick Dekker and I had been up since five a.m. looking for foxes. I had known Dick for years as a wildlife artist, author and researcher of wild canids and other predators. The two of us had seen nothing for three hours, but we were accustomed to such mornings. Patience is unquestionably a virtue for wildlife biologists. Now we sat with our spotting scopes at the edge of a farmer's field, watching the entrance of a fox den . . . waiting. Three days earlier Dick had watched four six-week-old fox kits (also called pups) romp and play around the den which had been dug under a small wooden granary.

Earlier that morning we had been discussing his theory concerning how coyotes avoid coming close to humans, their farm buildings and roads. Dick believes that red foxes understand the avoidance pattern shown by coyotes and, as a result, spend a large percentage of their time in this safe "no coyote zone," including locating their dens and raising their pups there. Coyotes and red foxes are competitors, and the larger, stronger coyote will kill a red fox if given a chance. Coyotes often shun certain areas because of reduced food supply or a high risk of persecution from humans. And it is these areas that are often inhabited by red foxes. Dick was the first researcher that I know of to document this interesting pattern of how coyotes and red foxes divide up the country. But more recently it has been documented by other researchers for many wild canids: red foxes and coyotes in the forests of Maine and Ontario, coyotes and swift foxes on the prairies of southern Alberta, and jackals and Blanford's foxes in the arid hills of Israel show this pattern, to mention just a few instances. It is one of the ways that foxes and their canid competitors—be they coyote, jackal or dingo—are able to co-exist in the same area.

We had just broken out our Thermos and sandwiches when two coyotes came out of the woods on the other side of the field. They got about one third of the way to the granary when a familiar cry broke the morning air. It was the high pitched alarm bark of an adult fox warning the pups to stay in the den. Obviously Dick and I were not the only two watchers out

and about on this early summer morning. Soon a red fox emerged from the woods, and Dick whispered to me, "It's the vixen." She was the mother of the four pups that he had been observing earlier.

As the coyotes kept walking toward the den, the vixen approached the coyotes, giving her shrill bark more frequently and more intensely. By the time the coyotes were a hundred yards (90 m) from the den, she was

30 yards (27 m) from the coyotes, pressing and baiting them. Suddenly the coyotes turned and dashed toward the vixen. She pivoted and started to flee toward the nearest edge of the woods. The chase continued in a hell-bent-for-leather manner, and it looked to us as if the coyotes were slowly narrowing the gap between them and the vixen. She ran in a zig-zag manner apparently trying to put distance between herself and her two pursuers. The coyotes, cutting some corners on the zig-zags, inched their way toward the vixen. When they were half-way across the field, however, things changed. The vixen seemed to throw it into high gear. Her neck became perfectly vertical; ears perked, she began to run with the litheness so characteristic of a red fox. Her paws ricocheted off the ground, and her bushy tail streamed behind her. She deftly put distance between herself and the two coyotes which by comparison were merely lumbering along.

Dick and I knew that coyotes could out-run most domestic dogs, but against this red fox these two seemed heavy-limbed and sluggish. We were once more reminded how graceful a fox is in full flight. The vixen ran back to the edge of the woods, stopped, turned, and intently watched the coyotes. They also stopped, and looked at her and at each other as if they were considering their options. Soon the vixen turned and disappeared into the woods, and the coyotes turned away from her and began to move along the edge of the woods. They walked along until they were once again opposite the den.

Then a strange thing happened. At this point, they separated: one coyote disappeared into the woods while the other animal started toward the den. I wondered what was going on. One coyote stayed out of view while its partner walked toward the den. When the coyote was about 300 yards (275 m) from the den, the vixen re-emerged from the woods across the field, and in a repeat performance, she began to bark and trot toward the coyote, baiting him to pursue. All the time there was no sign of the other coyote.

Again the vixen drew near, turning up the agitation of her alarm barking, trying to lure the coyote away from her den. Suddenly he did turn, as did the vixen, and the pursuit started again. However, the coyote was running differently now, running at an oblique angle, apparently trying to maneuver the vixen over toward the point of trees where his partner had disappeared. Dick and I tensed, wondering if their plans for an ambush would succeed.

The contest continued. Periodically the coyote stopped running, and the vixen stopped. The coyote turned and started back toward the den, and the vixen pressed him to pursue her. Then another chase occurred, the coyote trying to circle around the vixen slightly, herding her closer to that deathly edge of the woods. But try as he might, the coyote could not get the vixen closer than about 40 yards (36 m) to that point of trees. As the drama unfolded, it became clear to all concerned that the vixen had this situation well figured out. Finally the coyote hiding in the woods broke into open pursuit, but the vixen had kept a safe distance and now began to lead the two coyotes farther away from her den. Halfway across the field she once again threw it into high gear and distanced herself from the coyotes. The vixen stopped when she reached the edge of the woods, turned and looked at the coyotes, and then disappeared from view. The contest seemed decisive. Score: Red fox 2, Coyotes 0.

To say the least, Dick and I were impressed with how the vixen had handled the whole situation, and we praised her as we pored over the details, writing up the episode in our field notebooks. But the contest between these canid competitors is not always so one-sided: ten days later Dick found a dead fox pup at one of the entrances of the granary den. It was a kit with the marks of several canine teeth puncturing its chest. Shortly thereafter the parent foxes responded by moving their kits to a more isolated den. That move brought to an abrupt end Dick's observations on how this litter of fox kits was being raised. He searched for hours, in fact, days, to try to locate this family of foxes. All to no avail.

Further observations concerning how red foxes raise their young would have to wait a year, maybe two, until conditions happened to be right again—but that was all right. Naturalists learn to cherish the special moments in the lives of animals that they are privileged to observe; the rest is just part of the price that must be paid for the privilege. Sometimes I find it terribly frustrating; other times I try to reflect on the advice that a mythical fox once gave a young prince. Shortly before this fox disappeared on his little prince, the fox told him, "It is the time that you have wasted for your rose that makes your rose so important." Whether it is roses or foxes, on my good days I understand the wisdom of that advice.

*T*HREE
CANID *L*IFESTYLES

 No field experience has ever captured for me the basic differences between red foxes and coyotes as well as the one I had that summer morning. Although they are both members of the dog family Canidae, they are ecologically quite different species. The coyote is more cooperative and more social. Coyotes occupy a very different niche than the solitary red fox. In North America there are basically three different wild canids that occupy different niches: wolf, fox, and coyote. Their three predatory lifestyles have been tested by time and found to be ecologically sound. Furthermore, it is not a pattern unique to North America. On this planet, there are thirty-four species in the family Canidae, and most of them can roughly be grouped as "wolf," "fox," or "coyote" types. Specifically, this means that a wild canid survives and prospers by being a social predator of large prey ("wolf"), or they evolve into a specialized solitary predator of small prey ("fox"), or they evolve a lifestyle that spans the ground between the two ("coyote").

W O L F   This large wild canid is a social predator. Although opportunistic, it often hunts in a pack capturing large-bodied prey. The research of Canadian Wildlife Service (CWS) biologist Lu Carbyn on wolves in Jasper National Park is typical. In this region of the Rocky Mountains, wolves prefer to hunt deer wherever they are readily available. If not available, they turn to elk, and when elk are not available, they turn to moose. Hunting prey this large, however, is not without its dangers, and biologists occasionally observe wolves with broken jaws or cracked ribs from the prey kicking them, or wolves with their sides punctured by a horn or antler. As a result of these dangers, a wolf pack prefers to kill the smallest or weakest ungulate (a mammal with hooves) that is readily available. Wolves do prey on beavers and snowshoe hares, but over the long term, they need large-bodied ungulates as a major portion of their diet.

A pack of wolves is an impressive hunting team. In Wood Buffalo National Park in northern Canada, wolves hunt animals as large as free-ranging bison. Packs of up to twenty-five wolves work together, and by inflicting multiple small injuries, they on occasion kill even a mature male bison, usually by bleeding it to death. In this area an adult wolf averages approximately 100 pounds (45 kg) in body weight while a mature bull bison may weigh up to 2,000 pounds (900 kg). That's a size ratio of twenty to one. Wolves are able to accomplish this impressive predation by being sophisticated pack hunters. It is through cooperation that the pack is able to kill prey this large. Cooperation among members of the pack is useful in a number of other contexts; for example, defending a carcass from being usurped by other wolf packs, bears or cougars, as well as a pack working together to defend its territory against other wolves.

Through evolution, wolves' morphology (structure and form), physiology (bodily functions) and behaviors have been shaped to support their lifestyle. For example, compare a wolf skull with that of a coyote or red fox. Wolves have teeth that are stronger, more massive; they are also well anchored by their deep roots. Jaw muscles in the wolf are impressively developed. You can see these large jaw muscles reflected in the skull because of the large sagittal crest, a bony fin that appears on the top of wolf skulls near the back. The sagittal crest (which is where the main jaw muscles attach) is smaller on a coyote skull and almost absent on the skull of a fox.

A pack of wolves preying on ungulates leads a life of feast or famine. Wolves have evolved large stomachs in order to maximize food intake. Biologists have observed that an adult wolf can consume over 20 pounds (9 kg) of fresh meat at a single meal. On the other hand, biologists have also observed wolf packs going for ten to twelve days without making a kill. Especially during lean times, wolves make the most of each kill, using their strong teeth and powerful jaw muscles to crack the long limb bones of their prey and extract the rich marrow within. Or they can glean the last remaining protein and fat by gnawing the bones into a white powder.

The behaviors of wolves have also evolved to allow them to function as social pack hunters. For example, wolves have sophisticated communication displays. They snarl and show numerous subtle facial expressions that do not occur in solitary foxes. Wolves howl; foxes don't. A pack of wolves develops a complex social hierarchy with an alpha male and female assuming leadership roles. The alpha male of the pack decides when to move, what prey will be attacked, and what specific boundaries of the territory will be aggressively defended.

F O X   Foxes are not miniature wolves. They are specialized, solitary predators of small prey. Across North America, a jackrabbit is the largest prey that a red fox will hunt. A red fox weighs up to 15 pounds (7.0 kg)

while a jackrabbit weighs up to 10 pounds (4.5 kg). That's a ratio of two to three between prey and predator. Normally foxes do not hunt prey as large as themselves, and I do not know of any instances of foxes hunting as a pack—quite a contrast compared to wolves. These facts express that foxes are ecologically quite a different kind of predator.

Red foxes normally hunt a variety of prey—insects and other invertebrates; small burrowing mammals; rabbits and hares; and, to a lesser extent, ducks and small birds. Killing the small, alert, quick prey is the easy part; capturing them is the challenge for foxes. If any of these prey are given a second's warning, the fox goes hungry. Birds can fly up out of reach; squirrels can dash up a tree; rabbits and hares dart away often in a zig-zagging manner; and rodents can disappear under a log or rock or down one of their many burrows. Thus, foxes must hunt by stealth, capturing these alert prey in an almost catlike manner.

The largest amount of fresh meat that I have ever observed a red fox consume at a single meal is approximately 1.5 pounds (0.7 kg). That's approximately ten percent of its body weight, or proportionately half as much as wolves. Compared to banqueting wolves, red foxes are nibblers.

Red foxes seem to have "jumped" taxonomic families by evolving numerous convergent features with small cats, increasing their ability to hunt small prey. Red foxes' teeth are slender compared to wolves', and their canine teeth are especially catlike; that is, they are almost like daggers. Red foxes show many other catlike adaptations. For example, their front claws are semi-retractile, helping foxes to keep them sharp and to pin small burrowing mammals to the ground as an effective capturing technique.

Convergent evolution between the fox and the cat is striking in the anatomy of their eyes. Both animals have developed vertical-slit pupils and a highly developed tapetum lucidum. The latter is a glistening layer of tissue behind the retina that reflects light back out of the eye so that it passes over the retina twice instead of once. In photographic terms, the eyes of foxes and cats have a light multiplying device with a shutter that can stop way down to accommodate bright sunlight.

Foxes have also evolved many catlike behaviors, particularly in their hunting strategies. For instance, when hunting birds or tree squirrels, the red fox stalks with its belly almost touching the ground, or slink-runs from cover spot to cover spot, crouching and waiting for its chance to ambush the prey.

Among wild canids, only foxes show this cluster of feline features. Why have foxes become so catlike? The answer, I believe, can be found in the type of prey that they hunt. Foxes and small cat species are specialized predators of prey such as mice, voles and small birds. These prey naturally have evolved antipredator devices in order to avoid being eaten. As mentioned, these quarry have alertness and quick escape reactions, but they also show camouflage coloration, eyes on the sides of their head for wide-angle vision, and sensitive hearing in order to detect predators. To circumvent this arsenal of antipredator devices, foxes and cats have evolved in a strikingly similar manner.

C O Y O T E   Coyotes are less specialized predators compared to foxes or wolves. Coyotes have a more generalized canid body type and show a wide range of hunting behaviors. In certain circumstances, coyotes form packs and hunt cooperatively, taking down prey as large as adult mule deer. A male mule deer can weigh as much as 400 pounds (180 kg), and an adult coyote can weigh as much as 50 pounds (23 kg). That's an eight to one ratio between the size of the prey and the size of the predator. That's not bad, but still a far cry from Team Wolf.

On the other hand, coyotes can sustain themselves by capturing small prey if these quarry are plentiful. Like red foxes, they lunge after small burrowing mammals and pin them to the ground in order to capture them.

Red foxes have relatively light bodies, in part as an adaptation that allows them to perform long hunting lunges. I have watched a red fox on level ground, from a standing start, lunge 17 feet (5.2 m) through the air and pin a mouse to the ground. Coyotes, even though they are larger than foxes, have only been observed to lunge a maximum of 8 feet (2.5 m) in their attempts to capture these small mammals. In short, coyotes can hunt small prey but not as effectively as foxes.

Coyotes may not be specialized, but they are, above all, adaptable. This fact was brought home to me one day when I was tracking coyotes in fresh snow in the foothills of the Rocky Mountains. Three coyotes were spread out in a meadow, a hundred or so yards (90 m) from each other. Each one moved through the meadow, investigating shrubs and grass hummocks, walking along game trails searching for rodents and small birds in the nearby vegetation, and occasionally pouncing at prey. Very foxlike, I thought to myself. Then at a certain point, one of the coyotes

scared up a napping deer. The deer fled, and immediately the three coyotes fell into line behind one another and pursued. They chased the deer for over 200 yards (180 m), but then gave up the chase. Very wolflike, I thought. Then the coyotes spread back out across the face of this meadow, and each of them returned to the role of the solitary hunter. I was impressed. I had never seen such adaptable hunting strategies shown by either foxes or wolves.

THE DOG FAMILY   "Wolf" and "fox" and "coyote" are the three basic types of canids found around the globe. Most of the other species that make up the dog family Canidae have evolved to resemble one of these three viable forms.

"Wolves" are large social predators of large-bodied prey. They include the gray wolf, as well as the Cape hunting dog and Simien jackal of Africa and the dhole of India.

"Coyotes" are the adaptable middlemen of the dog family, occupying a flexible, opportunistic niche. They include the coyote and red wolf of North America; the golden, side-striped and black-backed jackals mainly of Africa; and several of the little known *Dusicyon* wild canids of South America. Domestic dogs, when they run wild or become feral normally support themselves as coyotelike hunters.

"Foxes" are the specialized predators of small prey and are represented by twenty-one species thriving in diverse habitats around the world.

CHAPTER 2

RED FOX:
THE VULPINE
SUCCESS STORY

 Various aspects of the life of the red fox have been shaped and sculptured by evolution to complement and support other aspects of its life. The end result is a whole that is greater than the sum of its parts: a canid species that has the widest geographical distribution of any carnivore alive in the world today.

By almost any criteria, the red fox *(Vulpes vulpes)* is a highly successful species. The red fox occupies most areas of the northern hemisphere, and it is expanding its range along a number of fronts: in northern Russia and Scandinavia, in the Arctic Islands of Canada, in the Middle East and in eastern Africa. The species is slowly dispersing into many new areas. During the mid-1800s, red foxes were introduced by English settlers into Australia, and they are flourishing throughout the southern and western regions. In fact, the red fox is so adaptable it can be found on four of the six continents—only South America and Antarctica have eluded its grasp.

FOOD HABITS The foundation of our understanding of the red fox should be based on something solid, and the fox's diet can serve well as a place to begin. Because of their elusiveness, carnivores are often notoriously difficult to study in their natural habitat. Many aspects of research on carnivores can be frustrating, but usually a field biologist is able to analyze what they leave behind, that is, their droppings or scats, to gain some understanding of what they eat. Several hundred food habit studies have been carried out on the red fox in many parts of the world.

Taken collectively, these studies repeatedly document two facts about the vulpine palate. First, the red fox's diet is best described as broad—the red fox eats a wide variety of food items, often sampling them according to their availability, and its diet changes from season to season. Second, while the fox will eat a wide variety of items over the course of a year, it relies on a limited number of plant and animal species as the real staples of its diet. On a year-round basis, small rodents, rabbits, insects, wild fruit and berries comprise most of the diet of the red fox. This research shows that the red fox obtains its food in one of two ways. The fox is a skillful scavenger, but it is also an efficient hunter. As a scavenger, the fox may utilize windfallen fruit, birds' eggs, winter-killed fish or carrion. As a predator, the fox specializes in capturing small prey. Scavenging and hunting are the mainstays of the red fox's lifestyle, combining to make this creature a most adaptable species.

Given the fox's varied diet and its small stomach, how does the fox handle problems of food shortage that will inevitably occur? Whenever the fox is in possession of surplus food, it carefully hides the provisions away for future use. The fox digs a shallow hole, pushes the food in, buries it, packs the dirt down and finally disguises it with leaves and twigs. Later, if the cache has not been robbed by another animal, the fox often locates the cache and eats its contents. The food caches of a fox may be particularly useful to it during times of food shortage or if the fox is injured and unable to hunt.

A SPECIALIZED HUNTER   The red fox is usually found to be nocturnal but also crepuscular, that is, active around dawn and dusk. The reason for this seems to be that these are the times when the fox's prey are most active; thus, the fox's activity patterns mirror those of its prey. During winter, when mice and voles become more active during daylight hours because they live in the twilight world underneath the snow, the fox becomes more diurnal (active during the day). In fact, the red fox in winter is active at various periods day and night around the clock.

The red fox's style of predation is even reflected in the evolution of its ears. A common pattern among many mammals, including humans, is that each species' sense of hearing is highly sensitive to the frequencies of its offspring's distress calls, but the red fox seems to be an exception to this widely documented rule. The fox's hearing is most sensitive to lower sounds.

These are frequencies that correspond to the rustling and gnawing sounds that small mammals make as they move through vegetation or chew on buds, seeds and twigs. Furthermore, Henrik Österholm, a Scandinavian researcher, has shown that foxes can locate these sounds to within inches of their true location, even when rodents are making these sounds under 2 feet (0.6 m) of insulating, fluffy snow.

To hunt these prey, the fox sits, cocking its head one way and then the other, triangulating on the sound until it can pinpoint it. Then the fox pounces, diving through the snow, trying to pin the small mammal to the ground under its forefeet. As a result of their finely tuned ears, red foxes are to be able to capture prey they have never seen but only heard moving under the snow or through dense undergrowth.

What constitutes prime habitat for the species is one more facet of the fox's lifestyle central to its hunting behavior. An insight into this question comes from watching how red foxes travel across the land. Populations of red foxes become most abundant in country that is varied—land that is made up of a patchwork of woodlots and open meadows, dense shrublands, pastures and small wetlands. The more diverse an area is, the more red foxes seem to thrive in it. Naturalist Ernest Thompson Seton described them as "animals of half open country." Diversified country is prime habitat for the red fox. Seton thought that varied countryside lends itself to the varied diet of the red fox. Seton was right, but there is another reason why foxes prosper in diverse habitat.

Another part of the explanation is that red foxes prefer to spend a disproportionate amount of their time traveling along the edge where two habitats meet; for example, where a forest and a meadow join. Numerous studies have shown that red foxes prefer edge environments. This preference can be understood by looking at the ecological links between vegetation, the fox's prey and the fox's hunting behavior. An ecological attribute of transition areas is that vegetation is denser and more diverse, because plants from both habitats are able to grow there. As a result of this lusher vegetation, small rodents, rabbits, birds and insects often find better food, shelter and nesting sites, and often become abundant. Naturally, red foxes tend to hunt where the prey is plentiful—and consequently are often observed to be "predators of the edge."

FAMILY TERRITORIES   If conditions are favorable, it takes surprisingly little prime habitat to support a family of

red foxes. David Macdonald, a British researcher, has documented that a family of foxes living in the rich farmland around Oxford, England, is able to support itself, living entirely within 25 acres (10 ha) of land. He found that the foxes could cross from one side of their territory to the other in only a matter of minutes, and yet they were content to stay within the boundaries of this territory for several years with no known sorties outside it. When food resources are less abundant or less predictable, it is more typical that about 3 square miles (8 sq km) of living space is required to support a family of red foxes. In the far North where food resources are periodically scarce and where Arctic winters bear down on the land, red foxes' territories sometimes expand to 40 square miles (104 sq km) in size.

Foxes usually divide up their countryside into family territories where the adults defend the area for their family's exclusive use. Field biologists thus have often found that each fox family exists on a well-defined, non-overlapping territory that the adult foxes, mainly the male fox, defend against other red foxes. Typically each territory contains a male (dog) fox, a female (vixen), and perhaps "helper" females from previous litters that assist in raising the next litter of fox kits born on the territory the next spring. Within this area, the foxes find enough food to support themselves and their offspring. The boundaries of the family territory are scent marked and actively defended, particularly in areas where food is abundant and less so in areas of food scarcity. This is the typical way that foxes organize themselves, but it doesn't do justice to the flexibility of the species.

RAISING YOUNG   Red foxes raise their young in a manner that is adapted to the fox's predatory lifestyle. In my northern study area, kits are born during late March or early April. In more southern areas, they can be born more than a month and a half earlier. When they are born, kits normally number between three and six and usually weigh less than a quarter of a pound (100 g). Fox kits grow slowly during the first few weeks, and their eyes do not open until they are ten or twelve days old. In southern areas, the vixen may leave the den after two days, but in northern areas, she stays constantly in the den from a few days before birth until the kits are approximately ten days old. She is completely dependent on the dog fox for food during this time.

Why the difference between northern and southern foxes? In northern areas, in late March the inside of the den is dank and the temperature at its warmest hovers around the freezing point. After measuring conditions inside a number of abandoned dens, it occurred to me that in northern areas the kits are so small and vulnerable during early life that the vixen must surround them with her warm body if they are to survive. The vixen might help to preheat the den before the pups are born, and then during their first two weeks she virtually forms a thermal blanket, protecting the kits in their frosty underground chamber.

When the cubs are a couple weeks old, the vixen begins spending more and more time away from the den hunting for herself, but she returns at regular intervals to nurse the pups. While she is there, she plays with the pups outside the den, and naps with them underground as well as grooms them, cleaning out their ears, licking their groins and eating their waste products. She continues these activities until the pups are about five weeks old and ready to be weaned.

The early life of a fox is not as carefree as one might imagine. At about twenty-five days of age, while the kits are still spending most of their time underground, they begin to fight viciously with each other in short, serious, and, in rare cases, fatal contests. If you listen closely, you can hear these fights taking place underground. Sometimes they break out aboveground as well. The fox kits fight on and off over the next ten days or so and, in the process, establish a strict dominance hierarchy. The alpha, or dominant, cub establishes itself, and the hierarchy continues all the way down to the omega, or most submissive, animal. This hierarchy among the kits determines access to food brought by the parents and dictates who can steal food from whom. If the parents are bringing in only a limited amount of prey (because prey is scarce on the family territory), the dominant pups get a larger proportion of the food and have the best chance of surviving, while the smaller and submissive ones may perish. The runt of the litter dies first, then the second lowest on the hierarchy and so on. It is a brutal process, but one that adjusts the size of the litter to food resources and maximizes the chances for the strongest pups to survive.

When the pups are four or five weeks old, they begin to come aboveground for longer periods. At this point, the hierarchy is solidly established and aggressiveness between the kits decreases and nearly disappears. They become more social, playful and puppylike. Over the next several weeks, the kits interact with one another and with their parents,

while hunting, fighting and food-caching behaviors develop. It is a wonderful time to observe wild foxes. The young foxes seem genetically programmed to try out these motor patterns in sessions of play fighting and play hunting, and it is fascinating to watch them practicing and perfecting these behaviors.

Food is distributed at the den by the parents in a vulpine ritual that is always the same. Carrying the food in its mouth, the adult fox arrives at the den, chortles a *"wuk-wuk-wuk,"* and one or more of the pups rush out. The first pup to approach the parent crouches low and beats its tail around wildly, whining and creeping toward the adult. Then, reaching up,

it smells, licks and bites at the corner of the adult's mouth. The adult gives the food to the first pup that begs for it. This seems to be the mechanism by which the food is more or less evenly distributed; however, once the pup has its food, its real problems begin. It now has to defend its prize against its litter mates. The kit tries to do this by running off or by threatening any sibling that comes near. Often, a dominant kit will challenge and steal the provision from one of its subordinate litter mates. On the other hand, two kits fighting over food will sometimes lose the prize to a sneakier sibling.

BECOMING ADULTS The family territory continues to play an important role in the pups' later development, allowing the pups to make the transition to adulthood in relatively safe and secure surroundings. The parents continue to bring food to the pups at the den until they are about three-and-a-half months old. Then an interesting change takes place. First the male and then the female start reducing the amount of food brought in. The young foxes seem content to play and horse around and be served food by the parents, but the parents make it clear that this is no longer an option. It is a difficult thing to prove scientifically, but from years of observation, I have come to believe parents start reducing food as a tactic to get the pups moving away from the den. Motivated by hunger, the kits start finding food on their own in the areas surrounding the den. At first the young foxes, even though they have gone on hunting trips with their parents, seem pretty scared and are inept at capturing prey.

In my northern study area, when the wild strawberries start to ripen, the parent foxes seem to start reducing the amount of food that they bring to the pups. Wild fruits, together with grasshoppers, crickets and other easily caught insect prey, form an important part of the diet of young foxes. Gradually the kits become more competent as predators and they learn that they have to hunt as solitary predators on the family territory. The slow transition to independence continues until the young foxes are about seven months old. It is at this point that the peace in the family begins to erode.

During September and October, a certain intolerance sets in between the dog fox and his male offspring, stressing the relationship until the young males leave the family territory and set out to search for mates and vacant territories of their own.

The fate of female offspring is more complicated. Young vixens may disperse from the family territory, but they usually do so in late autumn or early winter, a month or so after the young males have left. On the other hand, if conditions on the family territory are favorable, one—or in rare cases several—of the young vixens may stay on the territory for up to several years. Mother and daughters now form a strict dominance hierarchy with the older vixen in top position. The next winter the male fox and his mate breed and all the young vixens help to rear the kits. The subordinate vixens usually do not have litters of their own (unless food is quite abundant), but just serve as "helpers" to the dominant pair.

In years of abundant food supply, the dog fox may breed with not only the dominant vixen, but also with one or more of these "helper" vixens, and several litters of pups will be raised on the family territory. Thus, on rare occasions, biologists have observed pups from what are obviously two different litters being raised in the same den.

A SUCCESS STORY   It has always struck me that the various components of the red fox's life fit together like an intricate puzzle. It seems to me that each element of the fox's life is shaped by evolution to interlock and support other components of its life. The end product is a beautifully adapted creature—a small carnivore that is flexible and adaptable enough to occupy a diverse number of habitat types.

The picture that emerges is a life that fits together in an adaptive manner to create *Vulpes vulpes*, "the fox's fox," a slightly poetic translation of its scientific name. This is the red fox—a species that shows the widest geographic distribution of any carnivore alive in the world today.

CHAPTER *3*

$\mathcal{K}$IT $\mathcal{F}$OX: $\mathcal{T}$HE $\mathcal{D}$ESERT $\mathcal{F}$OX

 The kit fox and the swift fox are the Gemini foxes of North America. They share numerous ecological, physiological and morphological similarities, and there is even a scientific debate about whether these foxes represent one or two separate species. The kit fox and swift fox are North America's arid land foxes. They can usually be distinguished by their habitats. The kit fox (*Vulpes macrotis*) is ecologically adapted to desert shrub habitats of northwestern Mexico and the southwestern U.S. while the swift fox (*Vulpes velox*) thrives on the grassland prairies.

Both of these foxes are tan to soft gray, tinged with tannish orange on their legs and lower body. In their habitats, their coat color offers effective camouflage, especially under reduced light conditions from dusk to dawn when these foxes are most active.

Kit and swift foxes share many other attributes. Many of their body measurements are approximately twenty-five percent smaller than those found in the red fox. The kit fox is the smallest wild canid of North America, but the swift fox is a close second. Adult kit foxes weigh from 4 to 5.5 pounds (1.8 to 2.5 kg) while swift foxes are a bit heavier, weighing in at 4.5 to 6.5 pounds (2.0 to 3.0 kg). The body measurements of males from both of these species are on average about five percent larger than females, but these males often weigh nearly fifteen percent more than the vixens. The stockier build of the male is an attribute characteristic of many fox species.

Kit foxes often flaunt a slightly longer tail, one that averages sixty percent of its body length, as compared to the swift fox whose tail is only about half the length of its body. These two foxes show proportionately shorter legs than the red fox. Stubbier legs may be an adaptation for the distinctive zig-zagging run of which these foxes are masters. The trade-off is that these foxes are slightly slower than the red fox in flat-out speed, and they cannot lunge after prey as far as red foxes can.

Scientists have been debating for nearly four decades about whether the kit fox and swift fox are separate species. Much careful research has

been done to try to settle this debate, but it has yet to be resolved. On the one hand, recent morphometric research (detailed measurements of skulls and skeletons) as well as protein electrophoresis (study of proteins from animals to determine their genetic relatedness) support placing kit foxes and swift foxes in the same species. On the other hand, recent DNA fingerprinting analyses support the view that these foxes are two separate species.

What is abundantly clear is that these two foxes share numerous attributes, not only physical characteristics but ecological similarities as well.

LIFE IN THE DESERT   When the Spaniards first ventured into North America, they would have encountered kit foxes on all the North American deserts—Sonora, Chihuahua, Mojave and the Painted Desert, as well as the desert areas of the Great Basin. Unfortunately, kit foxes have been extirpated from much of their former range. Kit foxes are now extinct from Riverside and Los Angeles counties in California. The San Joaquin kit fox that inhabits all of central California is now recognized as a nationally endangered subspecies. In addition, Oregon has identified the kit fox as an endangered wildlife species throughout the eastern part of the state. In other areas, the kit fox thrives. In much of Nevada and western Utah, kit foxes are numerous and are often observed. In other areas, such as north-central Mexico and the Baja peninsula, we know kit foxes exist, but information on their numbers is virtually nonexistent.

Kit fox habitat is desert shrublands or desert grasslands. They seem to prefer flat, open areas and often inhabit areas where less than twenty percent of the ground is covered with any vegetation. Kit foxes differentiate between various desert habitat types and use them with discrimination. In western Arizona, a study carried out by a research team led by Bruce Zoellick, a U.S. Fish and Wildlife Service biologist, nicely documents this pattern in kit foxes. These foxes locate their dens in open areas containing mostly creosote bushes. The openness of these areas offers the foxes good visibility and protection against being ambushed by a coyote, bobcat or golden eagle.

On the other hand, the main prey of these foxes are nocturnal desert rodents such as kangaroo rats, wood rats and pocket mice. These desert rodents are most abundant in the denser vegetation that grows next to the dry beds of intermittent rivers and streams. At night, kit foxes move into these riparian habitats and do most of their hunting. They also hunt prey active in the daytime, such as cottontail rabbits, black-tailed jackrabbits and round-tailed ground squirrels as well as birds, but only when they happen to encounter these prey.

Within these areas kit foxes organize themselves in non-overlapping family territories where the size of the family and the size of the territory are determined by the abundance of prey. However, an interesting characteristic of kit foxes is that they defend relatively large territories—areas sufficiently large to provide for their families during droughts that occur periodically on the desert and have been known to last up to several years. On the desert, droughts set off a chain reaction in the food chain: Vegetation dies back, often causing drastic declines in the populations of insects, rodents and rabbits. After six to nine months, these events cause a significant decline in the populations of kit foxes and other predators.

Kit foxes show several lines of defense in response to prolonged desert droughts. During these times, fewer vixens breed, litters become smaller, and fewer pups survive to adulthood. Their large family territories help to provide at least a minimum of prey during these periods of drought. Interestingly, when the rains return and the desert blossoms and prey become abundant again, the territory of a kit fox family does not contract in size. Kit foxes continue to defend large territories apparently as insurance against future droughts.

Dens are an important component of the survival strategy of kit foxes. Both kit foxes and swift foxes spend the hottest part of the day sleeping in or near their subterranean homes; thus dens provide some protection from wind, storms, temperature extremes and moisture loss. As far as I know, Ernest Thompson Seton in 1929 was the first naturalist to call these foxes "the most subterranean foxes in existence," and it is a distinction which few have debated. Both species of foxes normally have fifteen or more dens on their family territory. Dens are useful for many purposes, such as resting during the day, taking shelter from storms, escaping from

predators, and raising pups.

As a strategy for protecting newborn kits, all foxes are experts at keeping a den looking quite abandoned, and these arid land foxes are no exception. To determine whether a den is being used by a fox, I very carefully locate all of the entrances to the den in question. Then I reach down several feet into each burrow and set up dried grasses in the form of a cross in each of these tunnels. A day or so later I check each of these entrances and if the grasses have been disturbed, it tells me that an animal the size of a fox has used this tunnel.

There is a field sign that can be used to recognize dens of both kit and swift foxes. These foxes do not accumulate a mound of dirt out in front of their entrances as do ground squirrels, gophers and other animals.

Arid land foxes scrape the dirt away from the entrance, spreading it out, so that there is normally a "tail" of excavated dirt spread about 10 feet (3 m) out in front of the den's entrance.

An interesting feature of the dens of kit foxes is that they are often not scattered at random, but are likely to occur in groups. Dens can be quite numerous at one or two locations of their family territories. As with arctic foxes, the vegetation in these preferred denning areas can be greener and more lush because of the accumulation of fox feces, prey remains and freshly excavated dirt. Abandoned kit fox dens often become important habitat for other desert species such as burrowing owls, antelope squirrels, lizards and various invertebrates.

NEVER DRINK, NEVER THIRSTY   All animals living in a desert environment must be able to exist on a stingy water budget. For animals, water balance is a matter of water–in and water–out. The extent that the kit fox has adapted to deserts is measured by the fact that it can exist for many months without ever taking a drink of water—an impressive feat! On average, a human needs to consume about 2.6 quarts (2.5 l) of water each day (some of which comes from moist foods and other liquids) in order to stay in water balance.

Foxes are not that different from humans when it comes to basic physiological processes. Kit foxes can exist in deserts because the sources of water that they depend upon come from the food they eat including the prey that they capture. Water that is derived from food is called metabolic water, and it comes in two forms—the water that is present in the food eaten by the fox as well as the water that is formed as the fox digests certain types of foods. During droughts prey often become the most readily available source of water for kit foxes. Thus kit foxes capture prey both for food value and as a water source. On average, an adult kit fox needs to have about 6 ounces (175 g) of fresh prey per day in order to stay in water balance. At certain times of the year, the prey needed for water content may exceed the prey needed for food content. At these times, a kit fox may be motivated to hunt more by thirst than hunger.

Kit foxes are quite good at this water conservation business. In fact, careful measurements have shown that through urination, defecation, normal breathing and panting, a kit fox loses only two-thirds as much water as expected for an animal of its size. We only partially understand how the kit fox is able to do this. However, use of dens, concentrated urine, dry feces, and a sophisticated panting mechanism that reduces water loss are all parts of its water conservation strategy. These are important attributes that help this desert fox survive.

DESERT SURVIVAL   Although the kit fox is the only desert fox found in North America, other arid regions of the world are inhabited by other desert or sand foxes. Understanding the extent to which foxes have adapted to the deserts of the world is to understand something of central importance in the evolution of foxes.

The twenty-one species of foxes found around the world are organized into three main groups: the thirteen vulpine fox species mainly of the

Northern Hemisphere; the seven little known *Dusicyon* foxes of South America; and the insectivorous bat-eared fox of southern and eastern Africa.

Nearly two-thirds of the vulpine foxes (8 out of 13 species) are desert foxes. Out of these species, four come from North Africa or the Middle East—the fennec, Blanford's fox, the pale sand fox and Ruppell's fox. The Cape fox occupies the Kalahari Desert and savannah areas of southern Africa. The corsac fox occurs widely across Central Asia, inhabiting steppes and semidesert regions. The Tibetan sand fox inhabits high plateaus and alpine desert areas of the Himalayan foothills. And in North America the kit fox inhabits northwestern Mexico and the southwestern United States.

The fascinating thing about desert foxes is that each species tends to exhibit the same cluster of impressive adaptations that allow them to cope with the harshness of the desert. This adaptive syndrome includes: a light-colored pelage for camouflage; largish ears for hunting insects and other prey as well as thermal regulation; highly concentrated urine, dry feces and other physiological mechanisms to reduce water loss; extensive use of dens on a year-round basis as protection against heat, wind, water loss, escape from predators as well as a safe place to raise their young; pigmented eyes to protect against solar glare; and often hair-covered feet as protection against heat and friction and to give traction in sifting sands.

Recent DNA fingerprinting research suggests that these desert adaptations arose and evolved on three separate occasions. This means that through the slow process of natural selection the same set of adaptations were "invented" and perfected three different times as foxes attempted to inhabit the various deserts of the world.

This cluster of adaptations needed to cope with the harshness of the desert has produced great similarities among these foxes. The fox and the desert have a special relationship: it is here through the slow, sculpturing process of evolution that some of the most fascinating foxes of the world have developed. Out of these remarkably adapted foxes, the kit fox is the only North American species to show a full set of the vulpine desert adaptations. As our only desert fox, the kit fox should be cherished.

CHAPTER *4*

SWIFT FOX: HOME ON THE RANGE — ONCE AGAIN

Rocked back and forth by the stiff prairie wind, I swayed over a hole in the ground. "She's gone!" I muttered. I couldn't believe it. No tinny beeps echoed in my earphones. I swept my antenna across the ground first in one direction then another. I adjusted the dials on my radio receiver and swept the antenna again. Nothing! Just dreaded static rang in my ears. I felt abandoned on the vast, windy prairie.

During the winter of 1985, I was working on the Swift Fox Reintroduction Project on the short-grass prairie of southeastern Alberta. For weeks, I had been keeping in touch with "Clarisse," locating her from radio signals emitted by her telemetry collar. Clarisse was a nine-month-old vixen, part of a highly valued swift fox lineage. Her parents had been born and raised in captivity at the Cochrane Wildlife Reserve, and then as adults they were painstakingly released onto the open prairie. Clarisse was one of their pups, their first litter born in the wild. As such, she represented hundreds of hours of care. I felt a heavy responsibility to find her. Yesterday she was here; she was sleeping underground in her den. I had confirmed that from her telemetry signal. Now she was gone; but gone where?

Was she dead? Recently a young dog fox and Clarisse had been denning together, and I had high hopes that they would have a litter of kits this spring. But two weeks ago a coyote had killed the male fox. Had Clarisse met the same fate last night? Maybe she had set off searching for a new mate. This is a fairly typical thing for a widowed vixen to do during the brown and dusty days of a waning prairie winter. I looked down at the den. Clarisse had used

55

this den religiously for weeks. I could always count on her. Especially on the windy days, after spending hours traveling across the prairies, I often saved radio-locating her for last in order to end my day on a positive note.

I looked around the open prairie. From the top of the small knoll where I stood, I could scan the horizon a hundred miles south across the impressive Milk River Canyon and up the slopes of Montana's Bearpaw Mountains. To the east, I could see past the Cypress Hills into Saskatchewan. Had Clarisse headed off in either of these directions? When a swift fox is underground my radio receiver can pick up a signal from 300 yards (275 m) away. If the fox is aboveground, I might get a signal from, at most, a mile away. In a land this large, such distances aren't even a drop in the bucket. The swift fox is a much smaller creature than most people realize. It is a buff or soft gray animal, tinged with orange, and about half the size of a red fox. Finding such a small carnivore cloaked in camouflage colors on the winter-worn prairies would be a challenge. I knew that my next several weeks would be spent criss-crossing countless miles of open prairie, searching for that tinny radio signal in my attempt to locate Clarisse. From past experience, I also knew that I had less than a fifty percent chance of ever finding her, either alive or dead.

DISAPPEARING ACT   One day three months later, to my total surprise, after I had searched long and hard over a considerable amount of prairie, Clarisse reappeared. As if out of nowhere, she returned to her old den—without mate or litter and certainly without offering me any explanation of where she had been. I was delighted to see her alive and, of course, asked for nothing else. Nevertheless my experience with Clarisse is a good illustration of the level of effort and frustration inherent in swift fox conservation.

The odds of re-establishing the swift fox on the Canadian prairies have never been high. It has been a conservation effort that has demanded infinite determination and inexhaustible patience. After more than two decades, however, the enduring swift fox is once again streaking across the plains of western Canada.

To understand this conservation saga, look at the historic distribution of this graceful, grassland species. Swift foxes (*Vulpes velox*) were found throughout the Great Plains region. Their native range extended from central Alberta southward through the Great Plains to west-central Texas.

Originally, swift foxes could be found in western Minnesota and Iowa clear to the foothills of the Rocky Mountains. But during the past century, the swift fox has disappeared from nearly two-thirds of its original range. In fact, the species is now restricted to a narrow north-south band from South Dakota to Texas. Like many endangered mammals, there is a good stable population toward the central region of its historic range—eastern Colorado and Wyoming—but it has become scarce in regions north, south, east or west of there. In fact, the last sighting of a swift fox in Canada occurred in 1938, and there it officially has been declared an extirpated species.

A number of interacting factors caused its disappearance. In the mid and late 1800s, the swift fox was heavily trapped for its soft, attractive pelt. Also for much of this century, predator-control programs for wolves and coyotes used bait laced with strychnine. This poison kills every animal that eats it. Unfortunately, wheat soaked in strychnine has been and still is being used to control gophers and prairie dogs on farms and ranches across the Great Plains. Because strychnine is a stable poison that is not metabolized inside an animal's body, when a rodent dies from this pesticide and is then eaten by a fox, the fox consumes all the poison in the rodent. If the fox scavenges several of these rodents, it does not take long for the fox to accumulate a lethal dose.

Loss of habitat has further contributed to the decline of the swift fox. As more and more land on the prairies is cultivated and native grasses are replaced by tall cereal crops, more of the prairies become useless to swift foxes. Furthermore, chemical sprays to control grasshoppers and other insect pests may selectively impact young foxes because these easily caught insect prey are important food resources when the pups first start hunting on their own.

ECOLOGY OF A PRAIRIE SPEEDSTER This fast and agile prairie fox is closely related to and similar in many ways to the kit fox. The ecology of the two species is remarkably similar. The two differ only by degree, but the differences are real nonetheless. The swift fox is an arid grassland species, not a desert dweller. Much of its range is the vast open prairie. In its habitat shrubs are rare, and swift foxes seem to prosper on flat plains with low ground cover where they can see a long way and move without restriction. Mixed-grass prairie with buffalo grass, blue grama, little bluestem and wire grass is excellent swift fox habitat.

The swift fox (as well as the kit fox) is more carnivorous in its diet than the red or gray fox. This predaceous tendency reflects the food resources that are readily available to each. Swift foxes are opportunistic predators, hunting off and on throughout the day and night. Their diet changes according to the prairie calendar. In spring and summer they depend on mice, eggs of ground-nesting birds, jackrabbits and, when abundant, young ground squirrels and prairie dogs. Grasshoppers, when plentiful, are eaten in great numbers. Autumn sees the swift fox harvesting wild fruits that grow within its reach, such as choke cherries or rose hips. Winter finds the swift fox scavenging on carcasses from livestock operations, roadkills or other sources. A whitetail jackrabbit is about the largest prey that a swift fox will hunt. It is a prey that on average weighs about 7 pounds (3 kg) compared to the swift fox weighing on average 5.5 pounds (2.5 kg). Here we have a case of a fox capturing a prey that is larger than itself—a rare occurrence in fox predation.

In the northern half of its range, the swift fox also has to cope with prairie winters. When a prairie blizzard is raging, these lands can be as cruel and life-threatening as the High Arctic. Prairie blizzards have frozen cattle in their tracks, engulfed telephone poles and stopped locomotives cold. The swift fox has to cope with near desert conditions in the summer and periodic prairie blizzards during winter. The swift fox is an animal that knows how to keep its head down. No wonder it is our most subterranean fox (although the kit fox would be a close second).

Swift foxes use dens not only for raising young but also for shelter from storms, protection from wind, heat and cold, reduction of moisture loss, and escape from predators. Swift foxes use their dens throughout the year, sleeping in the den or near its entrances. On many days of the year the mated pair share the same den, which is one of the reasons that swift foxes are judged to be slightly more social than the solitary red foxes.

Swift foxes suffer from a number of mortality factors—all of which reflect the changes that have taken place on the Great Plains during the past century. Coyotes in particular can wreak havoc on a struggling swift fox population. In our studies coyotes accounted for sixty-five percent of swift fox mortality where the cause of death could be determined. Wolves, the chief competitor of coyotes, have been exterminated from all the prairies and many other regions throughout North America. As wolves have been eliminated, coyotes have increased in numbers. Originally coyotes were found only on the plains, but today they have tripled their distribution and can be found from Alaska to Mexico. In addition, on the prairies populations of coyotes are believed to be much higher in number than before Europeans came on the scene. In many areas, coyotes may well be one of the major limiting factors that holds down existing swift fox populations.

SWIFT FOX CONSERVATION   The Great Plains of North America have changed remarkably during the course of the last century. In a very real sense it is one of the most altered landscapes on the face of the Earth. In many areas the unbroken sea of grass has been transformed into a geometric landscape—a puzzle of cultivated fields, each piece having its own hue and telling much about how it has been treated by its human stewards.

The great herds of bison have disappeared, the plains grizzly and prairie wolf have been exterminated. We may never fully understand the ecological niche that the swift fox once occupied on the native prairies. How did the swift fox interact with the huge herds of bison? What was its relationship to the plains grizzly or the prairie wolf? Did the swift fox have the same relationship to the grizzly and wolf that the arctic fox has to the polar bear? Did swift foxes trail along behind these large carnivores for much of the winter and scavenge scraps left over from their kills? Was this an important strategy for surviving prairie winters? We will never know. Many aspects of the original niche and habitat of the swift fox are likely to remain a mystery forever.

The challenge of swift fox conservation is to find out if the species can survive and prosper on the highly altered prairies of today. Is the swift fox doomed to extinction because its natural habitat has been so drastically altered? Or can it serve as a charismatic wildlife species, a conservation success story, that points out the need for widespread prairie restoration?

The efforts to bring the swift fox back from the edge of extinction on the northern prairies has been a conservation saga. After bone-numbing conservation efforts spanning decades, the swift fox can be sighted on the northern prairies once again. A similar program has been implemented with the kit fox in parts of the San Joaquin Valley in California. Both programs have experienced many of the same hardships and tribulations, and out of these conservation efforts important lessons have been learned.

The California kit fox conservation program is typical of the practical, multi-pronged approach that is often used for declining populations of free-ranging carnivores. In 1965, the State of California officially designated the kit fox to be a protected furbearer, and it was further declared a rare species under the California Endangered Species Act in 1970. Major penalties can now be enforced anywhere in California for shooting or trapping a kit fox or intentionally disrupting a den containing their offspring. In addition, surveys of active kit fox dens have been conducted annually, as have surveys of critical habitat, distribution limits, and estimates of adult population numbers. A large portion of the kit fox's range has been closed to night hunting, and aerial distribution of poisonous baits for vermin control is now closely supervised in all areas inhabited by kit foxes. Awareness of the beneficial aspects of kit foxes has been promoted in numerous education programs hosted throughout the kit fox's range. These efforts have helped. The rate of loss among kit fox populations has been slowed, but throughout the San Joaquin Valley and other areas of central California the kit fox remains a species threatened with extinction.

The conservation effort to re-establish the swift fox on the Canadian prairies has spanned more than twenty years and has involved countless professionals and volunteers: university researchers, government biologists, geneticists, veterinarians and many concerned citizens. In the two decades that this program has been active, it has progressed through three important stages.

During its first years, the team carefully assessed potential swift fox habitat. From historical records they had to predict where swift foxes might flourish. Miles and Beryl Smeeton—founders of the Cochrane Wildlife Reserve—learned how to breed and raise swift foxes in captivity. They then joined forces with University of Calgary wildlife ecologist Steve Herrero and others and started releasing captive-raised foxes in 1983 using a "soft release" technique. In this approach, researchers built pens on the release site and held captive-raised swift fox pairs for anywhere from six to nine months, feeding them daily. This soft release method was found to be very labor-intensive, and the survival of the foxes after release was disappointingly low.

The team then moved to a "hard release" approach where as many as twenty captive-raised foxes were released directly onto the prairies. No holding pens. No feeding program. Immediately, they were out there on their own. This was done because it was decided that habitat might be more important than release technique. The team found that prime release habitat invariably includes good escape terrain, an abundance of easily captured prey such as grasshoppers, and a low density of predators, especially coyotes. Good escape terrain simply means plenty of badger holes into which the swift foxes can escape from coyotes and golden eagles until they establish escape burrows of their own. This "hard release" technique has resulted in a greater percentage of the swift foxes surviving at least a year after release.

Recently, a third release technique has been developed. In the past few years the team has been releasing wild foxes in Canada that have been captured and translocated from central Wyoming. Since 1990, there have been four such releases, and the results are impressive. At the end of their

first year after release, almost half of the wild foxes still survived, compared with only eleven percent of the captive-raised foxes. Roughly eighty-five percent of the wild foxes gave birth to offspring during their first year after release, as compared with only twenty-five percent of the captive-raised foxes. Compared to captive-raised foxes, wild foxes survive better, reproduce more quickly and are considerably less costly to release. The team believes that this difference is due to the fact that the wild foxes are "street smart," that is, they have had a year or more of experience surviving in their natural habitat of Wyoming. They know how to recognize predators and avoid life-threatening situations. They also know how to capture prey and how to cope with severe weather conditions found on the prairies.

The net result of this prairie-size conservation program is that approximately 150 to 250 swift foxes are alive and thriving in the vicinity where the Alberta, Saskatchewan and U.S. borders meet. Many of these foxes have formed breeding pairs, and in years when prey is abundant, these fox pairs have raised more than fifty kits per year. It is a fragile start, but a good one. We are cautiously optimistic. Through considerable effort, swift foxes have begun to reclaim their home on the northern prairies after an absence of more than half a century.

CHAPTER 5

FOXES RAISING FOXES

by Shelley D. Pruss

Raising the pups is one of the most important things that foxes do, and various fox species do it somewhat differently. Wildlife ecologist Shelley Pruss from the University of Alberta has recently completed a two year study on how swift foxes raise their kits on the open plains. She shares some of her research findings here.

IN THE BLEAK MID-WINTER   For ardent red fox watchers, late January and early February may be the coldest time of the year but it can also be the most interesting. Courtship begins. The first clue is often the musky odor that permeates the woods around the fox's territory. Although both males and females develop this fragrance, it is particularly strong in the male's urine. Tracks in the snow that have been solitary for most of the winter suddenly become paired, indicating that the male and female are spending more time together. Finally, in preparation for the kits, the vixen cleans out several dens, one of which she will use for whelping.

About a month later, the swift fox—the smaller prairie cousin of the red fox—repeats the scenario. Living on the prairies as compared to the woods is one major difference between these two North American fox species. In both, the gestation period is short, about fifty-two days. At my latitude, red fox kits are born in late March or early April while the swift fox kits arrive a month later at the end of April or in early May. In both species, newborn fox kits are tiny, helpless and blind, relying solely on their parents for food and protection. A red fox litter of five is typical but may contain as many as nine hungry mouths. Swift foxes have litters that average four pups but can be as large as seven.

Why do red foxes court and give birth to their kits a month earlier than swift foxes, coyotes, or wolves that may inhabit the same area? Early whelping lets the red fox make maximum use of the numerous young snowshoe hares that are born starting in late winter. In addition, melting snow uncovers winter-killed carcasses which provide another source of food for red foxes.

On the other hand, the prairie-dwelling swift foxes do not give birth to their kits until early May when the birth of ground squirrels and other rodents ensure abundant food for the foxes. Or perhaps swift foxes whelp later in order to avoid becoming an early spring food source for coyotes. The differences in how swift foxes raise their young compared to red foxes are subtle but fascinating, and much remains to be learned.

CHOOSING A HOME   Little research had been done on how free-ranging swift foxes raise their young. So late one April I moved my tiny fiberglass trailer into a quiet swift fox neighborhood in the prairies of southern Alberta. On a typical day, I observed foxes between sunrise and sunset. On occasion, in order to document their 24-hour activity patterns, I would watch all night using a nightscope. Working about a hundred hours each week, my breaks were dictated by the foxes. During the midday heat they would disappear underground to nap in their cool, subterranean retreats. Meanwhile I tried to steal a few hours of sleep in my sweltering "microwave on wheels."

Having spent those afternoons in less than ideal accommodations, I began to be curious about how the foxes chose their homes. What, in a fox's eyes, makes a good den in which to give birth and begin to raise kits? Two obvious necessities for a suitable den are shelter from the elements and protection from predators. While an adult fox escaping a storm can use a simple hole in the ground, dens tend to be more carefully chosen when kits enter the picture. A good den is particularly important for the first four weeks when the vulnerable kits are almost exclusively underground. Not much is known about this stage in a swift fox's life. For now, researchers will have to surmise that similarities with the red fox exist and that some of the key points, like establishing a dominance hierarchy, hold true for both swift and red foxes.

The ideal family home ultimately depends on what kind of a fox you are. For example, red foxes typically inhabit multi-entranced whelping dens, dug in sandy loam on forested hillsides with easy access to a meadow and water source. Convenient access to water has obvious advantages. Sandy loam is simply easier for the foxes to dig in. Also, this soil combined with a hillside location and nearby meadow provides a place where the snow melts early and has excellent drainage. The surrounding forest provides shelter and escape; the adult foxes can sun themselves in the adjacent meadow, while they watch the exuberant kits at play.

OUT ON THE PRAIRIES   Historically, swift foxes were accurately described by early naturalists as one of the most "burrow-dependent" of all North American wild dogs. While the red fox often dens on hillsides, the swift fox frequently chooses den sites on the tops of the huge, rolling grass-covered hills. This provides swift foxes with the best possible view of the surrounding area. I never realized how critical this vantage point was until late one lazy June evening. Settled in my trailer near a hilltop den, I was busy taking notes as I watched the male swift fox take over "kit-sitting" from his mate. The male and the four kits ran and played among the prairie cactus.

Games of chase were interspersed with peaceful grooming sessions. During one quiet interlude, all the kits instantly disappeared. Half a second later the male shot over a hill and was gone. Before I could blink, a huge golden eagle swooped within inches of the den entrance and then soared off into the darkening sky. I rushed outside, peering into the gloom to see if the

eagle had a swift fox in its talons.

With no answers, I went back inside and waited. After twenty long minutes, the male's head peeked up over the ridge. One by one all four kits came up from the den and resumed their playtime with dad. I cheered silently and counted and recounted the kits to reassure myself that they were all safe. That incident made me realize the importance of the second or two of visual warning that may be gained by living on the top of a hill, whether the predator threatening to attack was an eagle, coyote or bobcat.

The choice of a den site is an important one, not only for shelter from storms, heat and cold but also from predators. A good den site is also a valuable commodity. In fact, many species of canids including kit foxes, arctic foxes, coyotes and wolves reuse existing den sites, although not always in consecutive years. Red foxes and swift foxes are also known to practice this behavior. One red fox den is known to have been active for nine of the last twelve years. Because adult foxes in the wild usually live only three to seven years, this den has likely been occupied by several generations of fox families. On the other hand, abandoned dens that have deteriorated through disuse may be fixed up and reused after long periods of vacancy.

TIME TO MOVE   For extra protection foxes never rely on just one den, and typically a number of burrows are hidden in a territory. Several factors may initiate a move between dens. If the vixen feels threatened or is disturbed, she may choose to move her pups to a new, safer den. Flooding of one or more of the den chambers may also force the foxes to leave. Some scientists speculate that once an area around the den looks too "lived in" with trampled vegetation and an accumulation of old bones and scats, it becomes conspicuous to predators, so the female will relocate her kits to a less disturbed site.

My first experience with kits being moved between dens occurred during one of the most torrential thunderstorms I have ever experienced on the prairies. Nearly 2-1/2 inches (60 mm) of rain fell that night amid crashing thunder and lightning so frequent that the sky was lit up more often than it was dark. In the morning the swift fox kits that I had been studying so diligently had been moved. Two weeks later, the foxes resettled into another den nearby. The initial move was probably caused by the den flooding, forcing the foxes to leave.

It was a rare privilege to watch this fox family move. Many members of the dog family grasp their young by the scruff of the neck, pick them up and carry them to a new den. However, this transport behavior is rarely seen in foxes, which tend to coax and lead their young to a new den. The actual process that the vixen used to move her kits between two dens (not much more than a hundred yards apart) took her over two hours. She tried to lure and entice the kits to follow her, but the kits reacted as if this move was quite a scary adventure—not to be undertaken lightly. She even used two fat ground squirrels as a treat to lure her litter to the new den. She would give a "gopher" to a kit, letting the pup play with it for a few minutes and then she would take it away and walk with it in her mouth toward the new den. After two stressful hours, with her kits safely underground in the new den, the vixen disappeared into the old den for a peaceful nap and was not seen again for seven hours.

THE MAN OF THE FAMILY   The role of the dog fox in raising the kits has been much debated among naturalists and field biologists. Some think that the male is never seen near the den site while others state that he is the primary provider of food for the kits. There is considerable variation among red foxes of different areas, the causes of which are not fully understood. However, red fox males studied in a fully protected national park environment have consistently been observed to bring food to the kits for at least their first ten weeks.

The data collected from wild swift foxes are consistent with those observations. The male was actively involved in providing food initially to the female and later to the young kits. But providing food was not his only job. He also groomed, guarded, and played with his young. Every evening just before nine p.m. the vixen would impatiently scan the horizon for any sight of her mate. Sure enough, within minutes, the male would trot home to the boisterous greetings of the vixen and kits. In fact, he was so devoted to his parental shift that I could almost set my watch by his arrival.

THE IMPORTANCE OF PLAY

Fox kits, like human children, seem to spend most of their waking life playing. Chasing, wrestling, leaping, pouncing, and stalking—their energy appears boundless. Sticks, cowpies, and old bones are often used for "tug-o-war" or for throwing high into the air merely to be caught again—often after a series of elaborate aerial contortions. The speed and grace of young foxes make me wonder if they are subject to the same laws of gravity as we humans are.

Several biologists have suggested that play is an important part of an animal's upbringing. One theory suggests that play helps young animals to learn and practice motor skills necessary for survival in later life. One of the most intriguing examples of this that I observed was a game that the swift fox kits played with their father. Toward the end of June, when the kits were about eight weeks old, a stalking game evolved. It usually began with a chase among the prairie grasses and pale yellow cactus flowers. Suddenly, the male would disappear into the grass. His body pressed flat to the ground with just the tips of his ears visible, the male would creep slowly toward a kit, periodically freezing when a kit was looking his way. The tiny kit, perched on a mound of dirt by the den entrance, would look about intently for dad until it was distracted by a nearby bird or grasshopper. Choosing the exact moment, dad would rush the kit, bowling it over and play fighting with it if the kit was not fast enough to escape down the den entrance.

As the kits grew older, their attention was not so easily diverted and they would often crouch down by the den quivering in anticipation, ears straining forward and their eyes locked on the male. With time and practice the kits became increasingly more successful at escaping by diving into the refuge of the den. This type of play suggests that the adult male was teaching the kits to be aware of and watch for predators as well as perhaps showing them how to stalk prey.

HELPERS   Although "helpers" have been observed frequently among red foxes they are not a part of the swift fox's family unit. It is not clearly understood why the difference exists. Perhaps the population density of swift foxes is now so low that all the young, dispersing foxes can find their own territory and consequently do not need to stay with their parents to acquire one. Perhaps future research may clarify why helpers have not been observed among swift foxes.

With or without helpers, another generation of foxes have been born and raised. They learn a remarkable number of things in just a few months, from how to be the hunter to how to avoid being the hunted. The kits that survive this difficult transition to adulthood leave to find a territory, a mate, and begin to raise their own families. The cycle is complete, and amid the blizzards of winter it will begin again.

CHAPTER 6

GRAY FOX:
THE FOX
THAT CLIMBS TREES

 One of my most vivid images of the gray fox was given to me while my family and I were traveling in Central America. One morning while I was having breakfast at a local cafe in one of the small rural villages of western Belize, I found myself entering into conversation with a young couple who occupied the table next to me. They talked enthusiastically about their trip to Guatemala to see the pyramids of Tikal. There, they had seen spider monkeys, toucans, and wild parrots in the jungle that surrounds the pyramids and makes up the Maya Biosphere Reserve, one of the largest protected areas in all of Central America.

They had climbed up the hundreds of steps of the Jaguar Temple with their Mayan guide in the pre-dawn light in order to watch the sun rise over the rain forest and pyramids of Tikal. Later they had climbed down through clouds of morning mist that hung in the jungle canopy. Half-way down, they spotted a small gray creature on the ground below. "*Gato de monte*," whispered their Mayan guide. It appeared to be a fox, carefully making its way along the base of the Jaguar Temple, intently searching and smelling between each huge block that made up the pyramid. The animal was dark gray in color, flecked with white, and they told me that the fox sported a black-tipped tail.

"It was a gray fox," I told them. "It's the only fox species found in this part of Central America." They described how it appeared to be searching for something to eat along the base of the pyramid; but, once it reached the corner of the temple, it lifted a leg, scent marked and walked away. It crossed an opening and began to investigate the edge of the dense jungle vegetation that grew there. They described how it walked along, carefully searching the vegetation for potential prey, and how silent were its movements. They watched it for ten minutes or so as it walked down a path, searching both sides of the trail, and twice during that time, it disappeared into the jungle only to re-emerge on the trail chewing what appeared to be some sticky tropical fruit. This was a fox that knew the jungle, an animal that could distinguish edible fruits from the ones that were unpalatable or poisonous. Finally the fox reached a curve in the trail and disappeared from view.

I listened intently to them describe their brief encounter with this gray fox. Their experience struck me as very expressive of the gray fox because it captured so well the elusiveness of the animal. We probably know less about the gray fox than any other fox species in North America. Its secretive nature and nocturnal habits make it a difficult wild canid to study. *Gato de monte* often eludes our grasp.

NOT CLOSE RELATIVES   In many aspects of its life, the gray fox appears to be strikingly similar to the red fox: food habits, reproductive biology, and many aspects of their behaviors are generally similar. These commonalities are so striking that one would expect these two fox species to be closely related species with the gray fox perhaps being a recent offshoot from the red fox. Not so, says the fossil record. The origins of the gray fox as a species appear to be more mysterious than that.

During the past decade or so, there have been several major research efforts aimed at scrutinizing the taxonomy of the dog family Canidae, simplifying it wherever it is scientifically justified. While a number of fox species have been brought into the genus *Vulpes* as a result of this research, the fossil evidence is simply too clear: the gray fox belongs in a distinct genus, *Urocyon*. It represents a separate evolutionary lineage which branched early from ancient canids and has existed as its own branch of the family for approximately four to six million years. DNA analyses further suggest that the gray fox is an old and well-established fox genus. It is interesting that gray foxes and red foxes are still so strikingly similar, given the amount of time that they have existed on different branches of the Canidae family tree.

In fact, it is the gray fox that has recently given rise to an offshoot, in the process forming a new species of fox. Gray foxes on six of the Santa Barbara Channel Islands, located 20 to 60 miles (30 to 100 km) off the coast of California, have been geographically isolated for several thousand years, allowing the fox population on these islands to evolve into a dwarf form of gray foxes. This smaller form of gray fox has occupied these islands for the past ten to sixteen thousand years. DNA analyses have identified several genes that are unique to these foxes, further supporting that they should be recognized as a separate species. Little is known about the ecology or behavior of these dwarf island foxes.

Consequently, the genus *Urocyon* contains two fox species: the Channel Island gray fox *(Urocyon littoralis)* occupies six small islands off the coast of California—as a species, it has the most restricted geographic distribution of any fox in the world; and the gray fox *(Urocyon cinereoargenteus)*, ranging from southern Canada to northern Venezuela and Columbia, excluding portions of mountainous northwestern United States, the Great Plains and eastern Honduras and Nicaragua.

IDENTIFYING GRAY FOXES   On average, the gray fox is about twenty percent smaller than the red fox. Adult gray foxes range from about 6 to 15 pounds (3 to 7 kg), males being slightly heavier than females. But it is the slightly shorter legs of the gray fox that make it look significantly smaller than the red fox. The gray fox is distinguished by three markings: its pepper-and-salt coat; the median black strip down the top surface of its bushy tail; and the black tip on its tail.

Interestingly, red foxes are not always red, but gray foxes are almost always gray. In other words, the coat color in gray foxes does not vary to the same extent as it does in red foxes. In many locales, the red fox shows three color phases—red, cross (red coat with a darkish strip down the back and across the shoulders), and black. These coat colors are genetically inherited just as eye color is in humans. Even within these three broad categories, foxes vary. Some red foxes are quite light and are called amber foxes. Many black foxes take on a silvery sheen during winter when long, silver-tipped guard hairs grow up through their summer coats. In winter, these foxes become silver foxes. The gray fox does not show this variation in coat color; its pepper-and-salt coat etched with orange is fairly uniform across its entire geographic range.

Not all identifying characteristics are readily visible. Another attribute of the gray fox is a large gland, located half-way down the top surface of the tail. All wild canids have this gland, called the supracaudal gland, but in the gray fox it is nearly twice as large as in other foxes, measuring 4.5 inches (11 cm) in length. In most fox species, this supracaudal gland gives off a strong musky odor, especially during the breeding season and while the adults are raising the young.

Even if a person out in the field only finds the skeleton of a dead fox, it is possible to tell whether it is a gray or red fox. At the top of the skull there are bony ridges over the eyes, called the temporal ridges. They join together near the back of the skull to form the sagittal crest. It is along these bony ridges and crest that the strong jaw muscles of a fox attach. From the top of the cranium, the temporal ridges on a red fox skull form a V-shaped pattern, whereas they form a U-shaped pattern on the skull of a gray fox. V for *Vulpes*; U for *Urocyon*. It's a useful and reliable field identification mark.

THE FOX FROM CENTRAL AMERICA   The gray fox is a southern fox species. The center of its distribution is Central America, and it occupies nearly all regions of Mexico and Central America. During the past fifty years, gray foxes have been sighted in many new northern areas—New England, Michigan, Minnesota, North and South Dakota, Nebraska, Kansas, Utah, and the southern parts of Ontario and Manitoba. On the surface these sightings seem to represent a recent, large range expansion of this species, but archaeological evidence tells a different story. Fossils from Pennsylvania document that the gray fox is not a recent immigrant to the eastern United States; it has occurred there for thousands of years. Fossils suggest that gray foxes arrived on Martha's Vineyard, an island off the coast of Massachusetts, about 1,500 years ago, but they were extirpated from the island shortly after Europeans arrived in the mid-1500s.

Early writings of colonists document that gray foxes were known to occur in southern Ontario and southern Maine during the middle of the 1600s. After that time they vanished and did not reappear in these areas until the middle of the twentieth century. The picture that is emerging from careful research is that as a species gray foxes expand their range northward during warm climatic eras, but its range contracts southward when cool climatic periods are combined with pressures from hunting and trapping.

One of the factors that may control the northern extent of its range is that gray foxes give birth to nearly hairless kits. These foxes normally give birth to their whelps sometime during April or early May. At birth, their kits are covered only by black skin while the kits of other North American canids are well furred. During April and May on the northern part of their range, the weather can be cool and the ground still frozen. Since hairless whelps born under these conditions may not survive, this reproductive constraint may limit the northern spread of gray foxes.

THE WHELPING SEASON   Many aspects of the reproductive biology of red and gray foxes are similar. In both species the vixen gives birth after a gestation period of approximately fifty-two days. The litter size is similar in both species but slightly smaller in gray foxes. They average four kits per litter as compared to the red fox's five. In both species, if the dog fox has survived the hunting and trapping seasons, he usually has an active role in helping to raise the young.

Gray fox vixens make a real effort to protect their newborn kits from the cold. As in the red fox, once the pups are born female gray foxes spend nearly all of the first couple weeks in the den wrapped around the pups keeping them warm. The movements of the vixen outside the den are quite restricted, and the dog fox provides her with most of her food during this vulnerable time.

There are interesting differences between where a red fox vixen chooses to give birth to her whelps as compared to a gray fox vixen. Red fox vixens normally give birth in a den that is dug into a hillside that is made out of sandy, loamy soil. Gray fox vixens frequently choose to give birth to their litter in earthen dens such as these, but they also choose locations rarely used by red foxes. Gray fox vixens raise their young pups in dens that are located in hollow logs, cavities in tree trunks, openings beneath boulder and rock piles, and even in sawdust piles and slabpiles located around abandoned sawmill sites. There are perhaps two reasons why gray foxes choose these denning sites that are rarely used by red foxes. First, these sites may, in fact, be warmer than dens dug into frozen soil. These dens may therefore increase the survival of the young, hairless pups. Second, gray foxes may use these types of dens because they are not as well-adapted for digging as red foxes are. The front claws of a gray fox are sharper, more curved and more retractile as compared to those of a red fox.

These are claws that are better adapted to other functions.

The propensity of gray foxes to den in sawdust and slabpiles has created an unusual relationship between these foxes and the forest industry. As timber operations have become more centralized and portable sawmills

have disappeared from most of our forests, sawdust and slabpiles have become rare, and gray foxes have lost these important denning habitats. Some wildlife biologists believe that the disappearance of sawmills has been a factor causing the decline of gray foxes in some areas.

A FOREST-ADAPTED FOX   Its curved, sharp claws distinguish the gray fox as a mammal adapted to the forest. Expressive of this fact is that the gray fox, until quite recently, was the only fox species known to climb trees. These foxes have been observed climbing trees by a number of researchers, and they do so under a number of contexts. Gray foxes climb trees to escape enemies, to rest in a safe, secure place, and also to harvest fruits as well as to pilfer eggs and young from a vulnerable bird's nest. The extent that gray foxes can climb trees is debated. Some biologists claim that gray foxes only climb trees that grow at a slant, so that the fox literally runs up the leaning trunk. There are, however, documented cases of gray foxes climbing vertical, branchless tree trunks to a height of 60 feet (18 m) by grasping the trunk with their forefeet and pushing with their hind feet. Gray foxes also climb trees by jumping from branch to branch, and they descend either by backing down a vertical trunk like a cat or by running headfirst down a sloping tree.

Adaptations for climbing are not limited to the gray fox's claws. Examining the anatomy of wild canids, University of California zoologist Milton Hildebrand documented that the gray fox was able to rotate its forearm like a cat or a bear. He concluded that this specialized motor skill was probably an adaptation for climbing.

When all of the evidence is considered, there is little doubt that this remarkable fox can climb trees and can do so quite effectively. It is not the only species of fox that is able to climb a tree, however. Recently, Memorial University ecologist Bohdan Sklepkovych observed several red foxes on Baccalieu Island, Newfoundland, climbing small balsam fir trees in order to eat cones during a winter of severe food shortage. He also observed a red fox 20 feet (6 m) up in a white birch tree, hopping from branch to branch. Such arboreal behavior in red foxes is, I believe, extremely rare, but it obviously does occur. Tree climbing in gray foxes, while not commonly seen, has been reported by a number of observers on many different occasions.

HABITAT CHOICES   Tree climbing is expressive of the gray fox's stronger preference for forests as compared to the red fox. Both species prosper in diverse habitat where fields and woods intermingle and where there is a mosaic of forests and farms. However, gray foxes spend a greater percentage of their time in forests, especially early successional woodlands, and are able to harvest food resources in the forest throughout the year while red foxes show a preference for edge environments.

Several studies have taken a detailed look at how gray foxes use different habitats. Not surprisingly, their use of habitat varies from one locale to another, but some common patterns do emerge. In southern Illinois and in southwestern Utah, gray foxes seem to favor recently abandoned hay fields and pastures. The foxes tend to avoid agricultural fields and brushy areas and use woodlands in proportion to their availability. In California, gray foxes also shun agricultural fields and favor woodlands and pastures. In areas of California where woodlands are restricted to forests along rivers and streams, the home ranges of gray foxes closely coincide with these riparian forests. In the Missouri Ozarks, the habitat use of gray foxes varies somewhat from these patterns. In this region, fields and non-forested areas are shunned by the foxes, and they favor mature oak-hickory forests more than any other habitat type.

A number of studies have found that dense vegetation is important as a daytime retreat for gray foxes. While gray foxes often spend much of the day in thick shrubs, they can be quite active in this brier patch, belying the claim that they are active only at night, dusk and dawn. In fact, it has been found that protective daytime cover is an important habitat requirement for gray foxes throughout their geographic range. Without this daytime retreat being available, gray fox populations in many areas have been observed to dwindle.

The gray fox is thus more of a forest species than any of the other foxes of North America. In fact, on a year-round basis, gray foxes are able to extract foods from early successional stands and even mature forests to a much greater extent than any of our other native fox species.

F O X   C O - E X I S T E N C E   Throughout the eastern United States and in many areas in the West, red foxes and gray foxes co-exist and probably have done so for thousands of years. How do these two fox species maintain themselves? Why doesn't one fox outcompete the other and gradually usurp its range? The Competitive Exclusion Principle is a principle of ecology that predicts that this is exactly what should happen. It says that no two species can have the same ecological niche and co-exist in the same area indefinitely; yet the red and gray fox appear to be quite similar. Specifically, how do these two fox species divide up the land and its resources?

Red foxes and gray foxes are repeatedly described as opportunistic foragers and predators of small prey where abundance and availability of food items determine the diet. While these overall similarities are true, there appear to be subtle differences in what each eats. Rabbits and small rodents are the dietary staples for both species, but red foxes seem to prey on these small mammals more frequently and supplement their diet with carrion, while gray foxes consume more plant material (such as corn and windfallen fruit) as well as invertebrates, particularly insects. In short, red foxes appear to be more carnivorous while gray foxes are more omnivorous. This slightly different emphasis in the diet of each of these fox species may help explain how they are able to co-exist in the same area.

Perhaps because of this slightly different orientation in their diet these foxes have evolved slightly different adaptations as well. Carolyn Jaslow of the University of Chicago recently examined this question, and her research on the anatomy of foxes has produced some fascinating results. She focused on a detailed examination of the teeth and jaws of these two fox species.

The species of the order Carnivora (that includes dogs, cats, hyenas, bears, raccoons, weasels, seals, mongoose and civets) are known for their predatory teeth. Almost without exception, the members of this order show well-developed canine teeth, often used for capturing and killing prey. Farther back in the jaws, the more predatory carnivores exhibit a pair of large meat-shearing teeth called the carnassial teeth. These carefully sculptured teeth slide by each other like blades of a strong pair of scissors and are used for cutting skin, ligaments and tendons as well as shearing muscle away from bones. Carnassial teeth are the equipment by which these carnivores butcher their prey.

Jaslow made extremely careful measurements on the skulls of gray and red foxes. She found that the teeth in the front part of the jaw are disproportionately larger in red foxes as compared to gray foxes. Yet the teeth in the back of the jaws of both species have proportionately remained the same size.

These physical features may give the red fox a wider gape for capturing and handling larger prey, and it may also give the red fox a quicker bite in order to capture swifter prey. In addition, red foxes exhibit larger carnassial teeth and stronger jaw muscles than gray foxes. These features may help a red fox more effectively shear meat off of carcasses, such as the remains of ungulates killed by wolves. Thus, these physical traits may make the red fox a more efficient carrion-feeder.

On the other hand, gray foxes show an expanded second upper molar that provides them with extra crushing surfaces for their omnivorous diet. In addition, gray foxes show an unusual prominence at the corner of their lower jaw, a subtle attribute that is only found in two other wild canids, both insect-eaters—the bat-eared fox of Africa and the raccoon dog of Asia. These two canids can chew extremely rapidly as a means of killing and crushing insect prey, some of which have highly venomous stings and bites. It may be that gray foxes are capable of these specialized chewing actions as well.

By feeding captive gray and red foxes different diets, Jaslow was also able to establish that gray foxes are able to extract more energy from fruits than red foxes can. On the other hand, both foxes are able to digest mice with about equal efficiency. So it seems that although red foxes and gray foxes superficially appear quite similar, the structure of their jaws and teeth and the physiology of their digestive systems suggest that each species has evolved different adaptations to deal with subtle differences in their diets. These adaptations probably help these two fox species utilize slightly different food resources and thus allow them to co-exist over a good portion of their North American range.

While certain aspects of the gray fox's ecology are understood fairly well, other dimensions of its lifestyle remain virtually unknown. The gray fox still remains the most elusive, least understood fox species in North America.

ARCTIC FOX: THE FOX THAT TRAVELS THE ICE

 I was standing on top of an abandoned fox den at two o'clock in the morning and could see for miles in any direction. Here on the arctic tundra, nothing grew high enough to block my view. The nearest tree was hundreds of miles south of me. At this hour, the sun was low in the sky, but the next sunset was still months away. The air was alive with golden, slanting sunlight that made the mosquitoes sparkle. I looked around—only the small hill and I cast shadows across the landscape. Fifty-three burrows punctuated the surface of the knoll, which was covered by lush green vegetation not evident on the surrounding, flat tundra. The greenness of this hill was due to the fertilizing effects of generations of fox droppings and the fresh earth excavated from the den.

Because permafrost (permanently frozen soil) comes so close to the surface of the ground in much of the Arctic, good natal den sites are rare. So rare that some biologists believe that the lack of den sites holds down arctic fox populations. Despite this, arctic foxes are still selective about where the vixens give birth to their pups. Dens are chosen in areas where there is little accumulation of snow, usually some protection from the severe winds, and a southern or western exposure that takes advantage of the heat of the sun. In northern Russia, researchers found that dens on south facing slopes became free of snow on average one-and-a-half months earlier than dens on north or east facing slopes.

Dens are usually located on small hills, slopes or river banks that offer good visibility in all directions. Stability of the surface during heavy rains as well as two or three feet of permafrost-free soil are also important attributes influencing where vixens locate their natal dens.

Once it is chosen, a natal den site can be used by vixens for the next three hundred years. Researchers find that such a den site usually passes through three stages in its so-called life cycle. From a youthful den with just one burrow into it, it progresses to a multi-entrance den, with some dens showing a hundred entrances dug into 100 square yards (84 sq m) of tundra. Finally, the burrows collapse and the den falls into disuse.

RAISING KITS ON THE TUNDRA   In early
to mid-April, the dog fox and vixen, which all winter long have been traveling on their own in search of food, now return to their summer breeding
territory. If the mate does not return, or if breeding for the first time, each
fox searches for a mate, a pair bond is formed, and, if needed, the pair
searches for a vacant territory with a good natal den site. In this underground chamber sometime in late May or early June, the vixen gives birth
to her litter.

The social organization of arctic foxes during the summer is quite similar to the family territories observed in red foxes year-round. During the
summer a mated pair of arctic foxes occupies and defends a family territory

that varies between 1 and 25 square miles (3 and 65 sq km) in size depending on food resources. Most of the time the family territory is occupied by one adult male together with one or more adult females. One female, usually the older dominant one, breeds and gives birth to a litter of kits on the family territory. The subordinate vixens act as helpers.

And help is needed! Arctic fox vixens give birth to impressively large litters, perhaps the largest litters of any wild mammal. On average, vixens give birth to ten or eleven pups, but when lemmings are plentiful on the tundra vixens have been observed to have as many as twenty-five pups in the same litter. Simply nursing these large litters presents the vixen with unusual challenges. One biologist was amazed to observe a vixen standing while thirteen of her pups nursed with such enthusiasm that periodically she was lifted entirely off the ground. In these very large litters, not all of the pups can nurse at the same time, and the competition for the available nipples can cause intense fights among litter mates.

The hungry pups start eating solid foods at three or four weeks of age, and they are completely weaned by the time they are two months old. It takes the collective efforts of the dog fox, vixen and any helper vixens to keep these pups supplied with food. In many areas of the North, most of the prey that the adult foxes bring to their young consist of lemmings. These lemmings can be about twice as large as a deer mouse or meadow vole from the South. Yet it takes about a hundred lemmings to satisfy the daily food requirements of a family of arctic foxes. In the Canadian Arctic, University of Saskatchewan ecologist Wayne Speller documented that a pair of breeding arctic foxes and their litter consumed approximately 18,000 lemmings during the ninety-day period while the young were being raised.

Adult arctic foxes are literally run off their feet supplying food to their large litter, and they often seem agitated and stressed during this time. In fact, in some northern regions, the fat deposits of adult arctic foxes peak in November and surprisingly are maintained throughout the long, dark, cold winter. However, these same fat reserves are badly depleted during spring and summer while the pups are being raised. Raising on average eight to twelve offspring takes a lot of energy.

RIGORS OF THE ARCTIC The ecosystems of the far North are simplified environments: only a small number of plant and animal species can cope with the harsh conditions of the Arctic. As a

result, the arctic fox depends upon a simplified diet, that is, a slightly small-er diversity of food resources, as compared to the red or gray fox. Over much of its circumpolar range, the main prey hunted by the arctic fox are lemmings and other small burrowing mammals. Other seasonally impor-tant food items for this fox are the eggs and young of both snow geese and brants; the eggs and young of colonial, cliff-nesting birds when arctic foxes can gain access to them; rock and willow ptarmigans; and carrion resulting from dead caribou, muskoxen or dead sea mammals found along the Arctic Coast. During late summer, arctic foxes also make use of crowberries and other berries that are plentiful in some areas of the Arctic. Arctic foxes also utilize food resources of marine coastal areas, and these foxes have been seen eating sea birds, fish stranded in tidal pools, marine invertebrates and seaweed.

The arctic fox is one of the many animal species in the North that has to cope with dramatically fluctuating food resources. Lemmings in North America do not commit mass suicide by throwing themselves into the sea as popular myths would suggest, but their populations do fluctuate dramatically, with their numbers oscillating by a factor of one hundred or more every four or five years. There is no doubt that lemming

populations cycle in the Arctic, and as a result, so do the predator populations. Populations of snowy owls, arctic foxes and jaegers cycle approximately a year behind these important prey. There can be a ten-fold fluctuation in the number of arctic foxes from one year to the next, with their peaks typically following the lemming peak by approximately a year.

How do arctic foxes survive this roller-coaster of resources? When food is plentiful, arctic foxes give birth to large litters, attempting to flood the next generation with their offspring. On the other hand, periods of food shortage cause severe die-offs or bottlenecks in the arctic fox population. When food is scarce, foxes respond in any, or all, of three ways. First, up to two thirds of the vixens fail to produce a litter. Second, in any given year a third of the yearling vixens do not breed; instead, they wait until their second or third birthdays before having their first litter of pups. Third, when vixens do give birth, even in years of scarce food resources, their litters are relatively large (ranging between five and fifteen pups). As in the red fox, arctic fox kits fight viciously at an early age, establishing a strict dominance hierarchy which determines access to the food brought in by the adult foxes. If food resources are scarce on the tundra that summer, the number of surviving kits is reduced to match food resources that the adults can supply.

The arctic fox is not a species that shows a long life expectancy. A study on Banks Island is typical. It showed that on average only fifty-eight percent of the adult foxes survive an arctic winter, with only one out of four juveniles surviving to their first birthday. Maximum recorded life span was six years for males and seven years for females, but only a small percentage of the foxes attain these ripe old ages.

Arctic fox populations are thus characterized by large turn-over rates. Cycling through these boom-and-bust patterns can have the effect of accelerating evolution in a species by subjecting it to severe environmental selection pressures. This appears to be the case with the arctic fox, resulting in a species highly adapted to harsh arctic conditions.

E V O L U T I O N   O F   A   S P E C I E S   Recent DNA analysis suggests that the genes of the arctic fox are distinctive enough to warrant placing the arctic fox in its own separate genus. Yet the arctic fox is one of the most recent fox species to come into existence. One theory states that the arctic fox (*Alopex lagopus*) evolved from the swift fox approximately 150,000 years ago. This is remarkably recent for a fox species that exhibits several unique adaptations. The glaciers were much farther south at that time. Swift foxes existing on the grasslands in front of the glaciers may have given rise to a mutant form of fox that was able to cope with the colder but highly productive lands found near the glaciers. These

ecosystems are cold, harsh environments but are very food-rich habitats. They are believed to have been the site of rapid evolution in a number of North American mammals, for example, mountain sheep, grizzly bears and wolves. Arctic foxes also may have originated and evolved as part of this rich ecosystem.

In its short history as a species, the arctic fox has achieved a broad circumpolar distribution, and has been characterized by rapid evolution, allowing it to adapt extremely well to challenging arctic conditions.

BLUE FOXES AND WHITE FOXES   There are two winter color phases of the arctic fox. In the white color phase the animal is typically pure white except for the black tip of the nose and its yellowish or dark eyes. The blue phase is a handsome brownish or slate gray during winter. In summer all arctic foxes have a much shorter coat that varies from gray or dark brown to black along the back and sides, but the belly and flanks are a cream or buff color. These coat colors are genetically determined, similar to hair color in humans. The white coat color is due to a pair of recessive genes. However, these coat colors do not appear at random in an arctic fox population, rather they are characteristic of two fairly different lifestyles found in the circumpolar arctic fox.

Arctic foxes inhabiting inland, colder areas predominantly sport a full white coat. In these areas, the ground is usually snow-covered for as long as ten months, and the white coat color provides effective camouflage. Blue foxes are typically found on small arctic islands or along the coast. Here, open seas reduce the snow cover of adjacent lands with the result that in coastal areas the slate gray color provides better camouflage. White and blue foxes actually exhibit quite different lifestyles. White foxes hunt lemmings, blue foxes make their living by beachcombing.

Biologists who have studied blue foxes find that they have a detailed knowledge of coastal features and make use of the richest concentrations of shoreline foods. Their knowledge of the coastline is impressive. Páll Hersteinsson from Oxford University completed a detailed field study of arctic foxes in Iceland. He documented that the foxes concentrate their visits to the shorelines starting three hours before low tide—the most productive time for them to go beachcombing. They had regular travel routes to the areas where there was abundant marine food, including mussels, stranded or injured fish, marine invertebrates and decomposing masses of seaweed infiltrated with growing maggots. Foxes that Hersteinsson studied were clearly able to predict periods of low tide as they changed from day to day and made use of this knowledge in their foraging activities.

LONG-DISTANCE HUNTERS   Arctic foxes tend to stay on their summer breeding territories as long as food resources are adequate. Some of the coastlines provide enough food so that foxes can inhabit these areas year-round, but not all arctic foxes are this

fortunate. Inland areas frequently do not provide adequate resources in the winter, and these foxes respond by making long-distance treks in search of food. Male offspring tend to leave first, dispersing in late summer, while female offspring and adult foxes start their long-distance travel in November or December.

A Russian researcher claimed that two-thirds of the arctic foxes in northern Russia migrate during the start of winter, approximately half of those heading south toward the boreal forest and the other half heading out onto the pack ice. Only a small percentage of these foxes ever return to their original territories.

During this season, arctic foxes often start trailing wolf packs and feeding on the remains of kills, or they travel far out onto the ice pack, following polar bears during the long arctic night, feeding on the remains of ringed seals killed by the bears. Foxes making these long winter treks in search of food can travel incredible distances. Arctic foxes tagged in western Russia have been recovered in northeastern Alaska. Arctic foxes have been sighted within 100 miles (160 km) of the North Pole, located in the most inaccessible parts of the ice pack. Arctic foxes will also migrate incredible distances south in search of food resources. They have been found at the mouth of the St. Lawrence River in eastern Quebec and within 95 miles (150 km) of the U.S. border in Manitoba.

Migration is a fundamental strategy for coping with the Arctic. Barren-ground caribou, polar bears, most arctic bird species and arctic foxes all perform impressive long distance movements in order to obtain essential resources to live in an immense, demanding land.

ADAPTATIONS TO THE COLD How do arctic foxes manage to cope with the paralyzing windstorms and temperatures that can hover around minus 50°F (-45°C) for weeks on end? In calm, windless conditions, a resting arctic fox in full winter coat does not begin to shiver (that is, expend energy to keep warm) until the air temperature reaches minus 50°F (-45°C). By comparison, red foxes are not nearly as well insulated. In calm air, a resting red fox begins to shiver at minus 9°F (-13°C). Arctic foxes exhibit a plethora of features that allow them to cope with the unrelenting northern winter. First, the body proportions of the arctic fox are all reduced in size compared to its southern counterparts. The arctic fox has a rounder, more compact head with a shorter muzzle; shorter, roundish ears; a short, compact neck; a shorter tail as well as shorter limbs.

Another striking difference between arctic foxes and red foxes is in the density of the arctic fox's underfur. Approximately seventy percent of the arctic fox's coat consists of a fine underwool—long strands of hair that coil and coil, creating a layer of dense fur next to the skin. In red foxes, only about twenty percent of the coat is underfur. In addition, arctic foxes produce a winter coat that is twice as long as their summer coat, and well-formed layers of fat provide further insulation.

Arctic foxes' paws, even the bottom surface, are densely covered in fur to reduce heat loss. Furthermore, arctic foxes, together with wolves, have evolved a set of adaptations that allow their paws to get quite cold without affecting their core body temperature. The paws of the arctic fox and wolf are just marginally above the freezing point during most of the winter. In part, this is accomplished by producing enzymes and muscle tissue that can function at these low temperatures.

In addition, a counter-current circulatory system is at work in their limbs. The artery that brings blood from the heart and descends the leg is surrounded by a lattice-work of veins ascending the entire length of the artery. As warm blood descends from the heart down the limb, cold blood ascends back toward the heart. Heat naturally moves from a warm object toward a cold object. The greater the temperature difference between the two, the more rapid the flow of heat. As a result, warm arterial blood is being cooled during its entire descent in the artery, and this heat warms the ascending blood. The efficiency is so good that the blood is near normal body temperature (98.6° F or 37° C) as it re-enters the fox's main body cavity. This is an expert design of bio-engineering evolved by arctic foxes, wolves and other animals. It not only greatly reduces the amount of heat loss, but also prevents the paws from icing up and developing abrasions and cuts during long winter travels.

Arctic foxes further reduce energy losses through their behaviors. When food shortages set in, an arctic fox seems to realize at an early stage that searching for food is unprofitable. It commonly seeks shelter in snow dens, thereby escaping low temperatures and strong winds. In these periods of enforced fasting, while it is denned up, its basal metabolism is reduced considerably in order to save energy. Consequently, the excellent insulation of its fur and fat, as well as the tucked and curled-up posture it assumes while sleeping, protect it from hypothermia during these prolonged periods of inactivity. Arctic foxes remain relatively alert during these times and can readily escape wolves or polar bears that may detect their whereabouts. Later, the arctic fox will move out of its den and try once again to locate food in the surrounding area. If it is able to find the carcass of a caribou or muskox, or if it kills a newborn seal pup in its snow lair, an arctic fox can replenish its dwindling fat reserves fairly quickly.

Clearly, evolution has molded the skeleton, physiology, reproductive biology and behavior of the arctic fox to allow it to prosper in the far North.

THE ROAD TO CONSERVATION Arctic

foxes have been able to adapt to the natural challenges of the Arctic more successfully than to the impact of human society. In its circumpolar distribution, the fate of the arctic fox runs the complete conservation gamut. On some Alaskan islands, arctic foxes were introduced and prospered, but are now unwanted. In Iceland, arctic foxes have been unwanted for the past eight hundred years. In Scandinavia and parts of Russia, native foxes were decimated, and now, late in the game, are highly valued. And finally, in Alaska and northern Canada, arctic fox populations are healthy, but the species is probably underappreciated.

In addition to coping with the pressures of human incursions, the arctic fox is also stressed by competition with the red fox. Despite the extensive evolution evident in the arctic fox, wherever arctic and red foxes co-inhabit the same areas, the outcome is clear: big rules little. Red foxes have repeatedly replaced arctic foxes in many northern areas. One such locale consists of islands off the west coast of Alaska—specifically the Pribilof Islands and some of the Aleutian Islands. Originally these islands were uninhabited by foxes. During the 1920s and 1930s when the price for fox pelts was high, arctic and red foxes were released onto these islands in an effort to "farm" these foxes.

Now, fifty years later, biologists are painfully aware of the havoc that these foxes have caused to the breeding bird populations native to these islands. However, despite twenty years of effort, these foxes cannot be exterminated. Nevertheless, one pattern is consistently seen. Typically when red foxes and arctic foxes compete, the red foxes consistently kill and replace arctic foxes. In fact, on two Aleutian Islands some sterilized red foxes were introduced in 1984 in an effort to eradicate arctic foxes. By the summer of 1992, some of the sterile red foxes remained on one of these islands, but the arctic foxes were absent from both.

In Iceland, the arctic fox is generally viewed with contempt for its supposed sheep-killing activities as well as damage to eider duck colonies. Legislation aimed at exterminating the species has been enforced by the world's oldest parliament, governing continuously since 1295 A.D. Despite eight hundred years of government-sponsored hunting and trapping of arctic foxes, their population still remained relatively high—until recently.

In the past few years Iceland has been experimenting with the release of sterilized adult male foxes from fox farms into the wild populations. These ranch foxes are usually larger than their wild counterparts, and are expected to dominate them. These sterilized arctic foxes may act as a biological control and may finally succeed in significantly reducing Iceland's arctic fox population.

In the coastal mountains of Norway and far northern Finland, arctic fox populations were high until the 1920s. Their numbers crashed through a combination of heavy harvesting pressures from trappers and food shortages from population cycles in their prey. Despite total protection of this species for over half a century, arctic fox populations have not recovered, and they are now regarded as threatened. The recent immigration of red

foxes into some of these areas is believed to be an important factor preventing the recovery of these arctic fox populations. Arctic foxes are also greatly reduced in number in many areas of Russia as red foxes expand their numbers northward.

The western and northern coasts of Alaska as well as the arctic tundra region of Canada still possess healthy, natural populations of arctic foxes. These populations fluctuate dramatically due to the four-year lemming cycle, but even in this continual state of flux, they probably represent the most natural populations of arctic foxes existing in the world. Populations from Iceland as well as North America have shown us that in areas where arctic foxes are not interacting with red foxes, arctic foxes can prosper even when their population is subjected to heavy hunting and trapping pressures from humans.

Northern Alaska and Arctic Canada offer the best chances for this species' long-term survival. These areas alone offer large tundra regions free of red foxes, where arctic fox populations can continue to follow their dramatic natural cycles as an important part of functioning arctic ecosystems. These northern jurisdictions thus have an important opportunity to conserve and protect this fascinating polar fox.

SPIRIT OF THE TUNDRA   Arctic foxes often strike me as little magic spirits of the tundra. I have been miles away from anything on flat, open tundra only to have an arctic fox mysteriously appear as if out of nowhere. I seem to feel an intense gaze at the back of my neck, and I turn around and there is an arctic fox studying me. It is a small, wispy predator. A number of researchers believe that the arctic fox is the most perfectly adapted of all arctic animals. It belongs to an exclusive northern clique that included muskoxen, polar bear, arctic hare, rock ptarmigan, and collared lemmings. It is difficult to measure evolutionary perfection among this elite group of wildlife species, but arctic foxes exist elegantly in areas where few other animals can survive. Their disappearance from any region is a great loss.

THE FUTURE OF FOXES

Foxes are intelligent, highly adaptable creatures. To conserve them need not be an onerous task. During the past several million years, they have coped with many environmental changes, often in remarkably successful ways. Small accommodations in the ways we use land could help foxes prosper into the next millenium.

The red fox is a remarkably successful species. It is one of those few, lucky wildlife species that has actually prospered in association with humans. It is not by chance that it is the carnivore species with the widest distribution of any alive in the world today. In fact, there are probably more red foxes alive now than at any other time. The symbiosis between humans and red foxes is largely a result of the fact that red foxes are "predators of the edge." Many human activities create openings and edges in the landscape. Woods are cleared to create agricultural fields, orchards, or to make room for houses and other buildings. Humans develop parks, golf courses, and airports as well as roads with miles and miles of edge environment. All these landscape changes inadvertently create prime hunting terrain for red foxes. As long as food is available and some shrubland or forest is left standing so that foxes can avoid enemies and find suitable habitat for dens, red foxes can prosper on these landscapes.

Gray foxes have also expanded their range. In the past fifty years, gray foxes have been sighted in many areas where they were not previously known. We don't know if these "new" areas represent true range expansions for the gray fox or a re-occupation of areas that they formerly inhabited during past centuries when the climate was warmer. New fossils would need to be discovered in order to answer this question. Whichever is the case, the gray fox, like the red fox, is certainly a widely distributed species that is doing reasonably well.

While red foxes and gray foxes are generally prospering, there are many areas where local populations of these species have been devastated. Wide use of pesticides for insect or rodent control, pollutants from manufacturing processes, and transformation of huge tracts of natural habitat into monocrop cultivated fields, shopping malls or urban sprawl have all taken their toll on local fox populations.

Another factor that adversely affects foxes is the price for furs. When the price for fox pelts increases, trapping and hunting efforts multiply, often with little regard for whether a local population of foxes is already depleted. Very few state wildlife agencies carry out an effective monitoring program that reliably indicates how abundant fox populations are.

Major advancements in fox conservation could be made by implementing small changes to hunting and trapping regulations. First, fox trapping and hunting seasons should close before the vixens start spending time at the den sites in anticipation of the birth of the kits. Taking an adult fox at this time of year basically means eliminating an entire fox family. Second, hunting seasons should be separated so that hunters pursuing, for example, white-tailed deer, are not able to simultaneously hunt for foxes. Finally, when foxes cause problems to domestic fowl or other livestock, specific fox families should be targeted where the adults are killed and the pups, if old enough, are removed from dens and transferred to other areas. Such an approach is more effective and humane than a bounty or control program inflicted on the foxes of that region. These are some of the simple changes that could be made to enhance the conservation of foxes.

The Channel Island gray fox has a remarkably restricted distribution—six of the Santa Barbara Channel Islands off the coast of California. Fortunately for this fox species, Channel Islands National Park was created by the U.S. National Park Service in the 1970s. The result is that most of the habitat occupied by this fox is protected within a national park. This is indeed a fortunate fox species! We still know remarkably little about the natural history of the Channel Islands gray fox, and research into its ecology, social organization and behavior is badly needed.

We tend to think of the arctic fox as inhabiting remote and isolated northern regions and existing virtually untouched by human societies. This is, however, a largely erroneous view. Arctic fox populations are doing well only on the western and northern coasts of Alaska and across the Arctic tundra of Canada. Only northern Alaska and Arctic Canada offer large tundra regions free of red foxes where arctic fox populations can continue to prosper.

If measures are not soon taken in the conservation of the arctic fox, I believe that we will see its slow, steady demise until its circumpolar distribution becomes highly fragmented, and we eventually lose this fascinating arctic species. It would indeed be a grievous loss.

There are still places where the swift fox and kit fox are holding their own. However, both species have vanished from large portions of their historic range. In many parts of their range, these foxes are clearly endangered wildlife species. Conservation programs trying to stem the tide are underway and are experiencing limited and hard-earned success.

There is an important message that the swift fox and kit fox give us about wildlife conservation in general: we have to be extremely careful with the wildlife populations that we have. It is a difficult and time-intensive undertaking to re-establish a wildlife population. When a species has gone extinct, it is clearly impossible to bring it back. A unique part of the Earth's biodiversity has been lost. However, these foxes show us that even re-establishing a population of a species, translocating animals from one area to another, can mean decades of strenuous work, with the chances of success often being meager. Wildlife populations do not transplant well. They are fragile resources. Their population structure and social organization have developed slowly over thousands of years, and once disrupted, these delicate entities are not quick to recover. It is far wiser to take care of the wildlife populations that are in existence than to try to restore them once they have been damaged.

This is the most important lesson learned from years of trying to reintroduce the swift fox to the Canadian prairies. It is a lesson learned by the people who are laboring for the recovery of the San Joaquin kit fox in California and by those in Scandinavia and Finland who have been working to bring the arctic fox back from the brink of extinction. It has been a lesson learned over and over again—in the tropical rain forests of Central America, on the savannas of Africa, and in many different kinds of habitat that are both near and remote from us.

We must learn to care for the natural heritage of the Earth, of which we are a part. Even if only for our own self-interest, we must preserve the wildlife that we have. For, ultimately, the way we treat our wildlife is the way we will end up treating ourselves.

Identifying Foxes

Although identifying foxes requires a little practice, it is not a difficult skill to develop.

There are many regions in North America where only one fox species inhabits the area. On the other hand, in much of the East and Midwest, red and gray foxes are likely to occur. In many areas of the West, red and gray foxes as well as kit or swift foxes can be found. There is even a region in the eastern half of New Mexico and adjacent parts of Texas where there are four native fox species.

Coyotes now inhabit all of North America except northern Quebec, the eastern half of the Northwest Territories and all the Arctic Islands. Unless you live in one of these northern regions, assume that coyotes inhabit your area.

When you see a small or medium-sized wild canid out in the field, the first thing to ask yourself is: Is it a coyote or a fox? The point to focus on is the fact that coyotes (as well as young wolves and feral dogs) are proportionately almost twice as heavy as foxes; they are not as lithe in their movements, and they seem to lumber along as compared to foxes. With a little practice, a person using these features can reliably identify foxes from these other canids.

If it is a fox, then focus on the tip of the tail. What color is that tip? That's the key. Red foxes normally flaunt a white tip. Swift and kit foxes show a black tip (as do coyotes). Arctic foxes show small, roundish ears and no contrasting color on the tip of the tail. Gray foxes sport a black stripe all the way down the top surface of the tail and then a black tip.

How do you distinguish swift foxes from kit foxes? Usually you can make the decision based on their range since the two species only overlap in the eastern half of New Mexico and adjacent parts of Texas. In short, kit foxes occur on the American deserts, and swift foxes inhabit the grasslands of the Great Plains.

If you are in doubt, focus on the ears of the fox. *Vulpes macrotis* means the "big eared fox," and the kit fox certainly earns this distinction. In the field, a fox with a black tip on its tail and largish ears will be a kit fox; one with a black tip on the tail and normal sized ears will be a swift fox.

These are reliable field signs which can help you identify which species of fox you are looking at. With a little practice, you can reliably identify any fox that you are lucky enough to spot.

RECOMMENDED READING

Allen, D. *Wolves of Minong: Their Vital Role in a Wildlife Community.* Boston: Houghton Mifflin Co., 1979.

Chapman, J. A. and G. A. Feldhamer (eds). *Wild Mammals of North America: Biology, Management and Economics.* Baltimore, MD: The Johns Hopkins University Press, 1982.

Henry, J. D. *How to Spot a Fox.* Shelburne, VT: Chapters Publishing Ltd., 1993.

Henry, J. D. *Red Fox: The Catlike Canine,* Revised Edition. Washington, D.C.: Smithsonian Institution Press, 1996.

Macdonald, D. W. *Running with the Fox.* New York: Facts on File, Inc., 1987.

Sheldon, J. W. *Wild Dogs: The Natural History of the Nondomestic Canidae.* New York: Academic Press, 1992.

SELECTED BIBLIOGRAPHY

Bailey, E. P. "Red foxes, *Vulpes vulpes,* as biological control agents for introduced arctic foxes, *Alopex lagopus,* on Alaskan islands." *Canadian Field-Naturalist* 106 (1992): 200-205.

Brechtel, S. H., L. N. Carbyn, D. Hjertaas and C. Mamo. "Canadian swift fox reintroduction feasibility study: 1989 to 1992." *Alberta Fish and Wildlife Report* (1993).

Doncaster, C. P. and D. W. Macdonald. "Optimum group size for defending heterogeneous distributions of resources: A model applied to red foxes, *Vulpes vulpes,* in Oxford City." *Journal of Theoretical Biology* 159 (1992): 189-198.

Dragoo, J. W., J. R. Choate, T. L. Yates and T. P. O'Farrell. "Evolutionary and taxonomic relationships among North American arid land foxes." *Journal of Mammalogy* (1990) 71: 318-322.

Egoscue, H. J. "*Vulpes velox.*" *Mammalian Species* 122 (1979): 1-5.

Frafjord, K. "Arctic fox, *Alopex lagopus,* home ranges and social behaviour in Svalbard." *Fauna* (Oslo) 48 (1995): 14-27.

Frafjord, K. and A. K. Hufthammer. "Subfossil records of the arctic fox (*Alopex lagopus)* compared to its present distribution in Norway." *Arctic* 47 (1994): 65-68.

Fritzell, E. K. and K. J. Haroldson. "*Urocyon cinereoargenteus.*" *Mammalian Species* 189 (1982): 1-8.

Geffen, E., A. Mercure, D. J. Girman, D. W. Macdonald and R. K. Wayne. "Phylogenetic relationships of the fox-like canids: Mitochondrial DNA restriction fragment, site and cytochrome *b* sequence analyses." *Journal of Zoology* (London) 228 (1992): 27-39.

Haroldson, K. J. and E. K. Fritzell. "Home ranges, activity, and habitat use by gray foxes in an oak-hickory forest." *Journal of Wildlife Management* 48 (1984): 222-227.

Harris, S. and J. M. V. Rayner. "Urban fox (*Vulpes vulpes*) population estimates and habitat requirements in several British cities." *Journal of Animal Ecology* 55 (1986): 575-591.

Henry, J. D. "Home again on the range." *Equinox* 13 (1995): 46-53.

Hersteinsson, P. and D. W. Macdonald. "Some comparisons between red and arctic foxes, *Vulpes vulpes* and *Alopex lagopus*, as revealed by radio tracking." *Symposium of the Zoological Society of London* 49 (1982): 259-289.

Hersteinsson, P., A. Angerbjörn, K. Frafjord and A. Kaikusalo. "The arctic fox in Fennoscandia and Iceland: Management problems." *Biological Conservation* 49 (1989): 67-81.

Hiruki, L. M., and I. Stirling. "Population dynamics of the arctic fox, *Alopex lagopus*, on Banks Island, Northwest Territories." *Canadian Field-Naturalist* 103 (1989): 380-387.

Jaslow, C. R. "Morphology and digestive efficiency of red foxes (*Vulpes vulpes*) and grey foxes (*Urocyon cinereoargenteus*) in relation to diet." *Canadian Journal of Zoology* 65 (1987): 72-79.

Lindström, E. R., H. Andrén, P. Angelstam, G. Cederlund, B. Hörnfeldt, L. Jäderberg, P. A. Lemnell, B. Martinsson, K. Sköld and J. E. Swenson. "Disease reveals the predator: Sarcoptic mange, red fox predation, and prey populations." *Ecology* 75 (1994): 1042-1049.

MacKenzie, D. "How Europe is winning its war against rabies." *New Scientist* 126 (1990): 26-27.

McGrew, J. C. "*Vulpes macrotis*." *Mammalian Species* 123 (1979): 1-6.

Nicholson, W. S., E. P. Hill and D. Briggs. "Denning, pup-rearing, and dispersal in the gray fox in east-central Alabama." *Journal of Wildlife Management* 49 (1985): 33-37.

Prestrud, P. "Adaptations by the arctic fox (*Alopex lagopus*) to the polar winter." *Arctic* 44 (1991): 132-138.

Prestrud, P., and K. Nilssen. "Fat deposition and seasonal variation in body composition of arctic foxes in Svalbard." *Journal of Wildlife Management* 56 (1992): 221-233.

Sargeant, A. B., S. H. Allen and J. O. Hastings. "Spatial relations between sympatric coyotes and red foxes in North Dakota." *Journal of Wildlife Management* 51 (1987): 285-293.

Savage, A. and C. Savage. *Wild Mammals of Western Canada*. Saskatoon, Saskatchewan, Canada: Prairie Books, 1981.

Seton, E. T. *Lives of Game Animals*. New York: Doubleday, 1929.

Sklepkovych, B. "Arboreal foraging by red foxes, *Vulpes vulpes*, during winter food shortage." *Canadian Field-Naturalist* 108(4) (1994): 479-481.

Wayne, R. K. "Molecular evolution of the dog family." *Trends in Genetics* 9 (1993): 218-224.

Wayne, R. K., S. B. George, D. Gilbert, P. W. Collins, S. D. Kovach, E. Girman and N. Lehman. "A morphologic and genetic study of the island fox, *Urocyon littoralis*." *Evolution* 45 (1991): 1849-1868.

White, P. J. and K. Ralls. "Reproduction and spacing patterns of kit foxes relative to changing prey availability." *Journal of Wildlife Management* 57 (1993): 861-867.

Zoellick, B. W. and N. S. Smith. "Size and spatial organization of home ranges of kit foxes in Arizona." *Journal of Mammalogy* 73 (1992): 83-88.